**John Harriss** in an emeritus professor of international studies at Simon Fraser University. He has also held teaching positions at the University of East Anglia and the London School of Economics, where he was a founder of the Development Studies Institute. He has held fellowships at the National University of Singapore and at the Centre for Modern Indian Studies of the University of Göttingen. In 2017, he was elected a Fellow of the Royal Society of Canada.

He has published extensively on various aspects of India's political economy, and is the author of widely cited books including *Capitalism and Peasant Farming* (1982); *Reinventing India: Liberalisation, Hindu Nationalism and Popular Democracy* (2000, with Stuart Corbridge); and *Depoliticizing Development: The World Bank and Social Capital* (2000).

# Liberty

*The Indian Story*

John Harriss

SPEAKING
TIGER

SPEAKING TIGER BOOKS LLP
125A, Ground Floor, Shahpur Jat, near Asiad Village,
New Delhi 110049

First published by Speaking Tiger Books 2024



ISBN: 978-93-5447-739-3
eISBN: 978-93-5447-738-6

10 9 8 7 6 5 4 3 2 1



Typeset in Garamond Premier Pro by SÜRYA, New Delhi
Printed at Chaman Enterprises, New Delhi

## Contents

# Introduction

*Harsh Mander*

In many protests around the country today, slogans are raised for *azaadi*. Azaadi means liberty or freedom. Freedom is indeed one of the most important promises of the Constitution. But what kinds of freedom, or azaadi, does the Constitution guarantee? It mandates freedom of thought, expression and belief. This means that every citizen is free to think, speak and believe in ideas which may not conform to the views of the government in power, or of the majority of people. In other words, it grants the freedom of conscience, the freedom to dissent, to disagree with power—political, social and economic power. Many believe that this freedom lies at the core of democracy.

The right to dissent must also carry the freedom from fear, the assurance that I will not be punished for holding beliefs different from those of the powerful. Rabindranath Tagore speaks glowingly of such a country, in which 'the mind is without fear, and the head is held high...'

History stands witness that it was only when brave women and men raised their voices against established orthodoxies of their time—when, say, Galileo said the world was round and not flat, or when Savitribai Phule and Fatima Sheikh established schools for girls when the kitchen was believed to be the only fitting confine for women, when Raja Ram Mohan Roy railed against a woman being burnt on her husband's pyre for *sati* or children being tied in marriage, when Babasaheb Ambedkar fought the idea and practice of caste in which the accident of your birth determines all your life chances, condemning you to a life of humiliation and discrimination, barring you from education and dignified work—that the world became a better place for later generations. We are here today because they refused to conform. Conformity leads to deadwood and regression. The freedom of conscience, the freedom to dissent, is therefore central to the pledge of liberty for all, which our constitution guarantees.

The Constitution also importantly assures the freedom of faith and worship. It protects the right of every person to follow her religion, her forms of worship, her ways of life including her choice of food and clothes. It allows people not just to follow but also to propagate their faith, and to establish their religious institutions.

There are other vital freedoms as well which are mandated by our constitution. These include the freedom to pursue the occupation we choose, to move to any part of the country and to form associations or unions, and of expression. This means the liberty to write and produce art, poetry, novels, books, philosophy, theatre, films—and video games and Instagram videos—which reflect our belief systems and our creativity.

As part of this series of short books that explain its principal ideas, John Harriss, a globally renowned scholar of India's political economy, writes luminously about the idea of liberty as mandated in the Constitution, and as imagined by those he refers to as the Founders—the authors of the Constitution and the leaders of our freedom struggle.

**India's Struggle for Freedom**

Mahatma Gandhi returned to India from the distant shores of South Africa in 1915. He was forty-five years old. The India he returned to, not unlike the one he had left as a young man, was mired in many unfreedoms, the primary one for a great many being political, enslaved as India was to rulers from across the seas for nearly two lightless centuries.

The colonial government could throw for years into prison people who rallied or fought against their rule. Some were hung from the gallows like the heroic young revolutionary, Bhagat Singh, some were banished for lifetimes to the distant Andaman Islands. Even those committed to peaceful, non-violent resistance to foreign rule were beaten back and often bundled into jail, sometimes for long periods of time.

The British colonized India because, at the time they arrived, this was one of the wealthiest and most industrialized countries in the world. In the two centuries of their rule, most industries had been destroyed, farming starved through rack-renting and artisans impoverished. There was misery and hunger in the famine-ravished countryside. The average lifespan of a common Indian was as low as 21 years at the time when Gandhiji returned to India.

The Indian people endured the agony of painful bondage in ways similar to the people of many countries in Asia, Africa and Latin America. A handful of Western countries had carved out large chunks of the globe, rich in natural resources. They devised various systems for arrogating the resources of these countries to their own ends: cotton for their mills, tea for their trade, land for their *lagaan*, food for their granaries, markets for their produce and soldiers for their wars.

The proud people of these enslaved countries, including India, rose heroically in revolt. All struggling people found their own pathways to freedom. What marks out our freedom struggle from most others was that the mainstream of our struggle was founded on the pivotal moral idea of *ahimsa*, or non-violence. Ahimsa means the resolve that I will fight you for my freedom and dignity, resolutely, accepting whatever consequences this battle will extract from me, including a bullet or banishment to prison; but even as I struggle against you for what is right and just, I will never hate you, and I will wish or cause you no injury or harm.

**A Broken, Wounded India**

The British eventually bent to the resilience of this struggle. However, they left not one but two nations—India and Pakistan. In frenzied riots on both sides of the new border which now suddenly separated sister from sister and brother from brother, a madness of hate seized the sub-continent. Hindus, Muslims and Sikhs slaughtered each other with a viciousness that cast a very dark and long shadow on the celebrations of freedom. Estimates of mortality range up to two million; an uncounted number were raped and abducted. Fourteen million people were cruelly uprooted from their homes, travelling often on foot, weary and heartbroken, for hundreds of kilometres, with their small children and the few belongings that they had been able to salvage on their aching backs. There is only one other distress migration, which humankind has witnessed in the course of recorded history, that was larger than this one. This was the forced trafficking of Africans as slaves to the Americas.

Pakistan was created as an independent nation for the Muslim people who lived in the west and east flanks of the teeming country. Its leaders urged Muslims in other parts of India to move to Pakistan to make this new nation their home.

There were some who advocated that India should be a country *only* for the Hindus—a Hindu India, a mirror image of a Muslim Pakistan. This would be a fitting reply to Pakistan, they felt, and would secure justice to India's overwhelming Hindu majority.

But Gandhiji had led our freedom struggle on the shining promise that India would be a country where people of every religion (or no religion!), caste, language and gender would be equal citizens in every way. Jawaharlal Nehru, India's first prime minister, declared that India would belong equally to all those who chose to make this their home, irrespective of their religion or community. One of Gandhi's closest associates, Maulana Azad, often spoke glowingly of his great pride, sense of ownership and resolute belonging to this country which he so loved. He declared that he was Muslim *and* he was Indian, and both these identities were inseparable from him, that he was willing to give up neither of these. He said India had given a great deal to its Muslim people, and the Muslim people too had given a great deal to their country. On 23 October 1947, as the country was reeling under the Partition, he stood tall on the ramparts of the grand Jama Masjid in Delhi and made a historic, heartfelt appeal to Muslims living in various parts of India to stay on, because this was their country and would always be.

This call was echoed over and over again by a Gandhi devastated to his soul by the tumult of religious hate and violence in India and Pakistan. He entreated Muslims over and over again to stay on in an India that he pledged would belong equally, in every way, to its Muslim citizens. A very large number of Muslims heeded his call, and the call of Maulana Azad and Jawaharlal Nehru, opting for multi-faith India over Muslim Pakistan.

When India was celebrating freedom in August 1947, however, Mahatma Gandhi was not in Delhi to celebrate as the Union Jack was lowered and the Indian Tricolour raised. He was instead in Calcutta, where Muslims and Hindus were killing each other in what appeared to be an unending bloodbath of hate. He went on an epic fast refusing to eat a morsel of food until the last of the violence had ended. He returned then to Delhi, trying to quell the hate and violence of hundreds of thousands of angry and sullen refugees separated forever from their homeland in what was now Pakistan. (These included my own extended family, uprooted from their birthplace.) He had planned then to travel (pointedly without a visa) into Pakistan to try to douse the fires of hatred that raged in this newly born country. But this was not to be.

Every day, Mahatma Gandhi would hold a prayer meeting, in which he recited prayers from all major religions. One of his favourite hymns included the line: '*Ishwar-Allah tero naam*'. On a winter evening on 30 January 1948, on his way to his prayer meeting, he was killed by a man violently opposed to his idea of an India which would belong equally to all people of all faiths. A stricken people mourned the death of the father of the nation, a man who paved the path to building a country which was humane and inclusive, which assured equal rights as citizens to people of every religion, caste, language and gender.

Babasaheb Ambedkar, who would lead the writing of India's constitution, had warned that any attempt to restrict India to people of the majority Hindu faith would be a 'calamity' for the nation and for democracy.

As the bullets of Gandhi's assassin signalled, not everyone shared this vision for India.

## The Constitution—a Dream, a Vision, a Set of Promises

Having shaken off the shackles of two hundred years of slavery in 1947, the Indian people chose to draw up the blueprint of the kind of country free India would be. Unlike several other countries that had newly gained independence around the time, India did not adopt wholly or partly a constitution left behind by the departing colonizer. The Indian people resolved proudly that they would write their own destiny, and they did so with solemn and searching reflection and debate for several years.

At the time of India's freedom, the world was still rebuilding and healing from the devastation and wounds left by the Second World War. The Holocaust had left around six million Jews, two-thirds of the entire Jewish people in Europe, dead, many in gas chambers built in Nazi Germany, the state led by Adolf Hitler from 1933 to 1945; along with multitudes of Roma and Sinti people, homosexual men, persons with disability and prisoners of war. The people of the world were learning from this horrific and tragic genocide the dangers of what happens in a country if minorities—religious, racial, ethnic, caste, sexual—are not protected. They were learning the cataclysmic consequences of the politics of hate and division. These were also lessons for the Indian people. The same lessons came out of the horrific Partition riots, and from India's epic freedom struggle.

Centuries of colonial bondage had reduced India from one of the wealthiest to one of the poorest countries of the world, in which famine, illiteracy, sickness and want stalked the countryside. For millennia, the cruel system of caste had made life a living hell for those unfortunate enough to be born into disadvantaged castes. Women were denied rights to property, education, work and dignity, and even sometimes life itself. Would we change all of this, and how? Who would this country belong to? Who would govern this country? How would the rulers be chosen? What powers would these rulers have? What powers and rights would the people have? And would the country's minorities—religious, caste, tribal and gender—be protected?

It was answers to questions like these that were written into the Constitution of newly independent India.

What is a constitution? It is a dream, a vision, a set of promises; a compendium of guarantees, a store-house of aspirations. It is a solemn articulation of the values that the country will hold close to its collective soul in its journey in the decades and centuries which lie ahead. It is the collective imagination of the destination which the country pledges to reach.

Most constitutions, except for those in the United Kingdom, Israel, Saudi Arabia and a few others, are written documents. The Constitution of India was written by a collective, the Constituent Assembly. They sat in the grand historic circular building which became for over seven decades the Parliament of the Indian republic. The Constituent Assembly had over three hundred members.

These women and men were, in a sense, the founding mothers and fathers of the Constitution. They were drawn from the people elected into the provincial assemblies of the time. And about a third were nominated, to ensure that those in attendance included people of every religion, caste, gender, culture, community and profession. The Constituent Assembly did not have members only from the Congress party which led India to freedom; members were invited even from parties strongly opposed to the Congress. One example is Babasaheb Bhimrao Ambedkar, who was the brave, charismatic and inspiring leader of the Scheduled Castes Federation, who had often stood in stout opposition to the Congress led by Gandhiji. Members of the Hindu Right were also invited to sit in the Constituent Assembly. There were many small kingdoms which were merged into the Indian nation, and their representatives were also members of this assembly.

Looking back today, we realize that it should have had many more women, more persons with disability, more Adivasi and Dalit people, many more working poor people, from factories and farms, and more gender minorities. But there's no denying the fact that the fine women and men who sat on the benches of the Constituent Assembly did indeed speak for all the people of India.

The first sittings of the Constituent Assembly began even before India became free, in the winter of 1946. The assembly deliberated for three years. A smaller group was carved out of the assembly called the Drafting Committee, which worked on the detailed draft of the constitution, and each of the sections of this draft were discussed in the assembly and then put to vote.

The chairperson of this drafting committee was one of the most learned men in the assembly, Dr Ambedkar, affectionately called Babasaheb. He contributed invaluably to many of the progressive measures written into our constitution. He was born into a very poor family of a soldier in the Indian army, from one of the most oppressed castes. On people from these castes for centuries was inflicted the most cruel form of discrimination which we know as untouchability. (Shamefully, that and many such practices endure in free India.) The country is fortunate that such a man—highly educated, wise and one who knew from personal experience the suffering of the most oppressed of our people—led the process of writing the Constitution. The two women members of the Drafting Committee, Hansa Mehta and Rajkumari Amrit Kaur, contributed spiritedly and thoughtfully to the deliberations, seeking to make the Constitution also reflect the aspirations of the forgotten and oppressed half of the population, women. We owe a lot to the founding mothers and fathers of the Constitution, who drew with us and for us the contours of the dream and the promise of a country based on equality and humanity which we resolved to build, one day.

From Mahatma Gandhi, we imbibed the idea and practice of radical love. From Babasaheb Ambedkar we learned the idea and practice of radical equality. These together became the cornerstones of our Constitution.

**Hum Log: We, the People of India**

Who indeed gave to us our constitution? The opening lines of the document answer this question. They tell us that 'We, the people of India' ('*Hum, Bharat ke log*') gave to ourselves this constitution. Who are 'we, the people of India'? We are the people who lived in this great and ancient land in past centuries; we are the people who were alive in India when the Constitution was framed; and we are the people of generations which followed and are still to follow. 'We' includes our grandparents and parents, it includes each of us who reside in this vast terrain today. And 'we' will include our children and their children one day.

The 'we' in 'we, the people' is the ocean in which many, many different little streams and mighty rivers meet. We derive strength and vitality from the plurality of our magnificent heritage. This kaleidoscope of our diversity is mirrored in our ever-changing natural features—from the Himalayas to the rivers, the forests to the deserts, the deltas to the plateaus, the coastlines to the islands. This kaleidoscope is made up of our music, of our art, of our dance forms, of our *gharanas* of classical music, and of their vibrant intermingling fusions. Of the spectacular range of our culinary choices, our varied taste buds that create a plethora of platters and cuisines, changing every few hundred miles. Of every festival of every religion and culture, which in our land becomes an Indian festival. Of our thousands of dialects and languages, such that if two people are selected at random from any ten in our country, chances are that they will speak different tongues.

India is the glorious symphony of our many different voices. It is a wondrous palette in which you can find every colour in the world, and we are privileged to be able to draw paintings of our lives from this multitude of colours.

All of these, all and every one of us, you and I, make 'we, the people'.

## The Preamble

The soul of the Constitution, its essence, is contained in a single page, which is called the Preamble. Every religion has a holy book, and prayer. Some people say that for the people of India, our holy book is our Constitution, and our prayer the Preamble.

But holy books are often placed on an unreachable pedestal; holy books cannot be questioned or changed. The Constitution is not that kind of holy book. It is a book which belongs to we, the people of India, one that protects and guides us through difficult times, but one that can be discussed, challenged and also collectively changed. It is a book of the people, not of the gods. It contains within it the values that the people of India pledge to uphold as the nation is built and as later generations come and go.

The Preamble first talks of the kind of country India will be. India will be sovereign, it says. This means its destiny will no longer be controlled by any foreign power. It will be democratic. This means its government will be chosen by its people. It will be a republic, which means that the ruler will not be born into power, in the way kings and queens have been born for centuries. Nor will the ruler snatch power through the bloodshed and brute force of military conquest or coups. The ruler will have to be elected by the people. Anyone, including those born into the greatest disadvantage, will have the right to aspire to become rulers, and seek the support of the people for the right to rule them.

An important question arose before the Constituent Assembly about which people should have the right to vote for their government. India became the first of the newly independent countries to give *every* person—man, woman or transgender, rich or poor, educated or uneducated—exactly equal political power to choose their rulers. One person, one vote. The richest and the most powerful man in the country would have the same single vote as the poorest, most destitute trans woman. A young person born in India today may think this is the most normal thing to do, but it wasn't at the time. It was a brave and radical—and some would say, audacious—idea. In Western democracies, for a long time only white men of wealth enjoyed the right to vote. Women had to fight long for an equal right to vote. In the United States of America, for instance, women got the right to vote only in 1920, and African Americans only in 1965. In Australia, aboriginal Australians did not get the right to vote until 1962. In India, the idea of universal suffrage for every person was adopted without any noteworthy dissent.

Many people had feared that Indians were not ready for this radical system of voting rights for all people, called universal adult franchise. Less than one in five people were even literate at the time of Independence; among women there were less than one in ten. But our founding mothers and fathers still resolved to place their faith in the ordinary Indian, even those denied education, wealth and social standing. They ensured that they would be guaranteed as their birth-right the opportunity to participate equally with every other Indian, the most wealthy, educated, socially or politically powerful, in choosing their governments, and through this, in building the nation and their collective destinies. For a society that would not allow the 'lower' castes to step inside schools and temples, to possess land,

and to live with dignity; for a society that would not allow some women even the chance to be born, let alone to own and inherit property and to work shoulder to shoulder with men—for this society to resolve to ensure the same and equal right to vote for every person, though not the end of the road, was a truly iridescent beginning to the great adventure of building a new nation.

From the first election in India in 1951, people from around the world watched with wonder and admiration as impoverished people, disadvantaged castes and women formed the longest lines outside polling booths. This has remained unchanged even until today. India's people of disadvantage are found to choose carefully and thoughtfully. The wonderment is that the people democracy has most let down are those who continue to have the greatest faith in this same democracy.

The Preamble goes on to mandate that the country will be socialist. This means many things. That the government must be committed to ensuring a decent standard of living for all its citizens. It must protect them from hunger and joblessness, and ensure equal and affordable education, health care, housing, decent work and social protection to all. It means a conscious state resolve to prevent the concentration of wealth in a few hands.

The Preamble also lays down that India will be a secular country. This means that the government will have no religion, and it will neither practise nor promote any particular religion. It will not discriminate in any way between people on the basis of their religion, whether they form a tiny minority of people, numbering not more than a few hundred people, following their traditional faith, or those who follow the religion of the largest majority of the Indian people. It also means that the state will promote harmony and goodwill between people with different belief systems.

In a particularly significant judgement of the Delhi High Court which decriminalized homosexuality in 2006, despite the stout opposition of people of almost every religious faith in the country, the bench declared that India's secular constitution gives every citizen of the country the freedom to follow their faith and beliefs. Of course, if their moral rules contradict the morality of the Constitution, it is constitutional morality that must prevail over individual religious beliefs. This ruling was first overturned by the Supreme Court, and then restored, but sexual minorities are still denied the equal right of people of the same sex to marry.

The Constitution promises equal justice to all people, in all aspects of their lives. Justice here does not simply mean what goes on in the courts. It means fairness. It means that people will not face discrimination in society because of their religion, caste, gender, sexuality or disability. They will not face discrimination in their participation in the economy, in work and in the markets. Women and men (and gay and trans people) will have equal access to employment, based only on their merit and not their gender, and will get equal pay for equal work. The ancient system of *begar*, or forced labour, imposed mostly on the most disadvantaged castes was abolished by the Constitution. No one could be kept as a bonded labourer. All persons are also to be treated fairly in their political life, when they go out to vote, to campaign, or to fight elections.

There are many ways that we are not equal. Some of us run faster than others, some cook better, some sing or dance or paint better, some score better marks in class, some can become mothers and others cannot, and so on. But above all of these differences, the Constitution recognizes us all to be equal in a fundamental way: we are equal in human dignity and human worth. There is, from this yardstick, no difference between the wealthiest person and someone begging for alms outside a temple or dargah. It is because of this inherent intrinsic equality that we all have an equal vote and equal rights and freedoms.

The Constitution requires that the government should ensure equality of opportunity. This means that wherever you might be born, in a village, a slum, the city streets or a mansion, you are entitled to the same opportunities to study, in the same quality school or college, and the same chances to develop your potential, whether for intellectual pursuit, sports, music, art or anything else. It also requires governments to ensure equality of status. This is an even more difficult task. It means that at least to some degree, governments must ensure more equal conditions of life to those who are more disadvantaged. This can only be done by what is called redistribution, by taxing the wealthy to ensure the right to a decent life to the disadvantaged; and by reservations or affirmative action, which recognizes that people who have for centuries been treated unequally need special support in education and jobs for them to achieve real equality in the conditions of their lives.

The Constitution also firmly and categorically bans the practice of untouchability. This—along with the principle of one person, one vote—are arguably the most radical sections of the Constitution. It outlaws unambiguously a practice that has brutalized and shamed Indian society for at least two millennia. Untouchability is one of the most troubling, cruel and disgraceful parts of India's historical legacy. By the accident of birth into a particular caste, it condemns people to a life where they are not allowed into religious shrines, share food or water with other people who will avoid so much as their touch, and will prevent them from walking on the same road as them or riding a horse in a wedding procession, or studying in school or college. The Constitution prohibited these shameful practices. This provision transforms the Constitution, at least in part, into a luminous moral document, seeking to confront and atone for the crimes of our history.

After liberty—which I speak of in the beginning, and which is the subject of this volume—justice and equality, the fourth pillar of the Constitution is fraternity. Fraternity in English means brotherhood. This must of course include sisterhood as well. The Hindi version of the Constitution uses the beautiful word *bandhuta*. Derived from Sanskrit, this means the idea that we are bound to and with each other. Looking at it in another way, *bandhu* means friend, so bandhuta can also be understood as an ideology of friendship.

Fraternity or bandhuta encompasses the lustrous idea that we might have between us enormous differences—of wealth, gender, caste, religion, language, ability, the colour of our skins, the size of our eyes and noses, who we choose to love and marry, the food we eat, the clothes we wear, and so much else—but are *bound to and with each other* despite that. We are brothers, sisters, friends.

Dr Ambedkar rightly said that the most important idea in the Constitution is the idea of fraternity. It is this idea which affirms the equal dignity of every individual. We learn from him that the other foundational ideas of the Constitution can be conceivably accomplished even if there is no fraternity. But this would be possible only by enforcing these through the strong arm of the state. However, if there is fraternity in society, then you don't need the state to enforce justice, liberty, equality: instead, these become the natural order of things.

Bandhuta is therefore the single most precious idea of the Constitution, but also the hardest to accomplish. So many people teach us hate—our leaders, our peers, our elders, our heroes from films and sports, our friends. We need instead teachers, leaders, philosophers, writers, film-makers, singers, artists, friends and family who teach us love.

Remember, it is not a country founded on hate, fear, division and inequality which we, the people of India promised to build. The country we gave to ourselves was a humane and equal country founded on love. Bandhuta is what brings us together as one country. We are not one country because we are alike. We are one country because, despite every difference in the way we look, eat, dress, speak, worship, love and think, we belong to and with each other. If there are shackles on your feet, I feel my freedom has been stolen. If you sleep hungry, I am unable to sleep. If your suffer loss and pain, tears well up in my eyes.

**Our Reality**

But what is our reality? Look around. It is apparent that 'we, the people of India' have built a country still far distant from the India we promised ourselves in our constitution. And in some ways this distance is only growing.

Think of which of the magnificent and solemn pledges that we made to ourselves have been realized. What has become of the dreams of our founding mothers and fathers?

A great deal has indeed been accomplished. Every person in this country continues to hold the power to choose her government. Citizens of a large majority of newly independent countries were denied or lost this power, to military coups and dictators. Fewer people in our country are poor, fewer sleep hungry than when we won our freedom. The average length of life has risen from 37 years in 1947 to 67 years three quarters of a century later. We have some fine institutions for teaching the humanities, engineering, medicine and management, our warehouses are overloaded with food grains, we are the IT back office of the world, and our cities glitter with gated colonies, luxury cars and crowded malls.

But look carefully, and you will find that one in every third child is still malnourished. This means that their bodies and brains are not allowed to develop to full potential for lack of nutritious food and clean water. Children of the poor study in separate, significantly less resourced schools than children of the rich. Many are not allowed to study at all, and instead parents still feel compelled to send them out to hard labour. Every second woman is anaemic. Eight out of ten doctors in India work for for-profit private hospitals, and government spending on health care in India is among the lowest in the world. If poor people fall ill, they cannot rely on good quality publicly provisioned health care. Wealth accumulates in an incredibly small numbers of hands, and this is barely taxed. At the other far end of the spectrum, nine out of ten workers toil in casual, insecure, unsafe jobs at dirt wages. As they age, most have barely enough pensions to secure their aging with dignity and health care.

People still suffer horrible violence and discrimination because of their religion, caste and gender; or because they walk the paths of equality that is their right; or when they choose to love and marry outside the socially prescribed boundaries of religion, caste and gender. Adivasis are dispossessed by large powerful corporations from their forests and homelands, and are branded as Maoists and jailed when they protest. Crowds gather and lynch Muslim and Dalit men, beating them to death, and proudly videograph these crimes and circulate these on social media. Untouchability continues with pitiless and ferocious violence. Dalits are beaten and killed in India even today for growing a moustache, for building a two-storied house, for asking for fair wages, for just advancing in life through their own hard work and talent; their children thrashed for drinking water from an earthen pot meant for their 'high-caste' teacher. And these horrific crimes are rarely punished.

Governments punish instead people who disagree with them. The freedom to dissent is dying, with fear and official targeting choking voices of truth. The freedom of religious faith is threatened by the politics of majoritarian hate. People spend years in prison because they are too poor to afford legal counsel, because the courts are clogged and uncaring, because they belong to stigmatized religious and caste identities, or simply because they dare to challenge the injustices of the state.

Reflect on the essence, the morality, the soul of our constitution. It is not perfect. With the hindsight of history, there are some things we might want to change. But contained in it are the iridescent dreams we had for this nation when it threw off its chains of slavery. These are the ambitions, the lofty and worthy goals that we, the people set for our country. And since these are promises which we have made unto ourselves, it is for you and I, 'we, the people of India', to rebuild this country into the kind, equal, free and just land imagined by our founding mothers and fathers.

We must build with the bricks of our hearts and minds, of our dreams and our struggles, of our accomplishments and our sacrifices, and I hope, of love.

## This Series

India recently celebrated seventy-five years of its Independence. As one small tribute to the Indian freedom struggle, we propose a series of ten books that summarize in simple, accessible language the core values, imagination and pledges of the Constitution. The themes for these books we have been drawn mainly from the Preamble—Secularism, Socialism, Democracy, Justice, Liberty, Equality, Fraternity. In addition, we include the themes Scientific Temper and Federalism; these too are essential to the morality of the Indian Constitution. We are fortunate that the fine minds and hearts who we approached—some senior, some younger—all agreed generously to contribute to this series.

These books draw from the Constituent Assembly debates, and indeed from those that preceded them. Each book also looks at how these ideas evolved in independent India, through court rulings and executive actions. The series also looks at the relevance of these ideas to the challenges of the India of today, the extent to which the state, the polity, the economy and society remain faithful to these ideas, the principal contestations to these ideas, and finally, the ways in which these ideas are important for India's future as a humane, democratic state.

Dr Neera Chandhoke, one of India's leading political scientists, and Distinguished Fellow of the Centre for

Equity Studies, consented to help me bring out the series and has also written the opening book for it. Ravi Singh, co-founder of Speaking Tiger and one of India's finest editors, agreed to publish this series. We hope to get these translated into Hindi and other Indian languages as well.

At a time when the morality and pledges of the Constitution are under assault, it is our fervent wish that this small project—an effort to unpack and popularize it—will be useful as resistance, defence and public affirmation of the luminous morality of the founding document of India.

Where the mind is without fear and the head is held high, into that heaven of freedom let my countrymen awake

—Rabindranath Tagore

# Author's Preface

The aim of this small book is to reflect upon, and—hopefully—to encourage thought and debate about one of the cardinal values of the Constitution of India: Liberty. This vitally important idea appears, of course, prominently in the Preamble to the Constitution, which states the intention that the sovereign, democratic republic of India will secure to all its citizens:

> JUSTICE, social, economic and political;
>
> LIBERTY of thought, expression, belief, faith and worship;
>
> EQUALITY of status and of opportunity; and to promote among them all
>
> FRATERNITY assuring the dignity of the individual and the unity and integrity of the Nation of India

Rabindranath Tagore, in the statement that I have taken as the epigraph, refers however, to 'freedom', rather than to 'liberty'. The Constitution, too, often speaks of 'freedom'—as it does in Article 19 that refers to freedoms of speech and expression, of assembly and association, residence, movement and vocation—rather than of 'liberty'. As I explain in chapter one, these two words, in English, are usually understood as meaning the same thing—essentially, 'the state or fact of not being subject to despotic or autocratic control, or to a foreign power'. But I argue that the idea of 'liberty'—which comes from Latin—has certain connotations that can be seen as distinguishing it from 'freedom', which came into English from Old German. 'Liberty' has associations with the broad political philosophy of liberalism—the two English words have the same Latin root—and it is understood as connoting the freedom of individuals to make their own choices and to pursue their own courses of action, exercising their personal, political and property rights. Liberalism generally holds that individual freedom is inherently associated with the right to private property.

These ideas were certainly important to those I refer to as the 'Founders'—the leaders of the struggle for freedom from colonial rule, and the men and the few women who were the members of the Constituent Assembly that was responsible for drawing up the Constitution between December 1946 and 1950. Granville Austin, author of the classic study on the making of the Constitution, who drew on interviews with a fair number of members of the

Assembly, as well as on transcripts of the debates and on papers of the various committees, argued that 20 members constituted the most influential group. Seventeen of them were Hindus—nine of them Brahmins and one a Dalit—while two were Muslims and one a Christian. Twelve were lawyers. Among them, Austin thought, four outstanding leaders of the Congress—Jawaharlal Nehru, the prime minister; Vallabhai Patel, home minister and deputy prime minister; Rajendra Prasad, the president of the Constituent Assembly; and Maulana Azad—formed an oligarchy within the Assembly. They enjoyed exceptional authority, deriving from their roles in the struggle for freedom from colonial rule. Dr B.R. Ambedkar, the Dalit leader, an astute lawyer and a learned man, was also particularly influential. Among other roles that he held, he was the chairman of the Drafting Committee, and has often been described as the architect of the Constitution. On one occasion a member of the Assembly said of him: 'The whole House is useless unless Dr Ambedkar agrees'*—though on some crucial matters, as I explain in the book, Dr Ambedkar did not get his way. I might also single out the eminent lawyer Alladi Krishnaswamy Ayyar, and K.M. Munshi, both of whom played particularly important parts as members of the Drafting Committee, and in the debates, and the

* Naziruddin Ahmed, 28 December 1948.

Constitutional Adviser, B.N. Rau (not a member of the Assembly), whose influence was considerable, as I also explain.

Many of the Founders were deeply influenced by the ideas and values of liberalism. Nonetheless, as I argue in chapter one of the book, I believe that the concept of liberty, or freedom—*azaadi* in Hindi/Urdu—that animated their deliberations, and that is advanced in the Constitution, may be seen as going beyond the liberal conception. The Founders certainly were concerned to ensure that Indian citizens should be free in precisely the sense of 'not being subject to despotic or autocratic control', and the individual freedoms valued by liberals are set out in Part III—the Fundamental Rights. Chapter two of this book provides a discussion of these provisions of the Constitution. But the Founders also sought to establish what Jawaharlal Nehru once spoke of before the Constituent Assembly as 'real freedom'—which would allow Indians to live in social and economic conditions that provide for their dignity and independence. These conditions are set out as responsibilities of the state in Part IV of the Constitution—the Directive Principles of State Policy, which as I argue in chapter two, can be seen as setting out an agenda for the social democracy that Dr Ambedkar believed would be necessary for sustaining political democracy.

Given this understanding of the meanings of liberty, or freedom, in the Constitution, chapter three of the book concerns the debates that took place in the Constituent Assembly over the Fundamental Rights, and how these rights were whittled down through the policies and actions of successive governments as they 'worked' the Constitution (Austin's phrasing), in the years after it came into force. In part, this came about because individual liberties, and especially the right to property, were found to hamper the realization of the societal transformation that the achievement of 'real freedom' required. But more significant, and increasingly so, were what were perceived as, or thought to be, the needs of national security and of 'the unity and integrity of the Nation of India', spoken of in the Preamble. In this history I see Article 22 of the Constitution, which refers to the powers of the state to use the instrument of preventive detention, as a kind of 'Trojan Horse' (the device used by the attacking Greeks of the Ancient World to enter the city of Troy). It has had the effect of making possible the curtailment of the liberties set out especially in Articles 19 and 21 of the Constitution, on which I focus. These articles, with Article 14, on equality before the law, were described by one Chief Justice of India, Yeshwant Vishnu Chandrachud, as a 'golden triangle', standing 'between the heaven of freedom into which Tagore wanted his country to awake and the abyss of unrestrained power'. They have been seriously weakened, however, as governments have adopted ever more repressive measures. This has especially come about in the first two decades of the 21st century, as I discuss in chapter five, notably with the consolidation of the majoritarian rule of the Bharatiya Janata Party after 2014—even though not beginning with it.

Chapter four of the book, which follows a brief account of observations on the experience of liberty, especially in India's villages, discusses the progress that has been made towards the realization of the 'real freedom' of which Nehru spoke. Though the precursors of the Constitution, the draft constitution set out by the Motilal Nehru Committee in 1928 and the Karachi Resolution of the Congress of 1931, argued for certain economic and social rights, these radical proposals were not taken up in the Constitution of 1950, which substituted for them the Directive Principles. Progress has been made, no doubt, through the life of independent India, towards the realization of the objectives set out in the Directive Principles. This is shown in the extent to which abject poverty has been alleviated. But still, the pattern of the country's development has meant that the ambition of the Founders has been disappointed. The 'new rights agenda' that was fostered by the United Progressive Alliance government between 2004 and 2014 made for some advances, but far too many Indians continue to lead lives on the edge of poverty, largely excluded as they are from productive employment. In significant part this is because of the egregious failures of successive governments to deliver quality education for all, and accessible, effective health care. Without these, Nehru's ambition for free India, that it should be possible for every Indian to have 'the fullest opportunity to develop himself according to his capacity', will continue to be disappointed.

In the last chapter, chapter five, I comment on the 'legalized lawlessness' that seems to characterize the actions of the Indian state, thanks in good measure to the way that the police functions, and I show how freedoms—both positive and negative—have been diminished in contemporary India. It is hard to avoid the conclusion that the country has now slipped into the 'abyss of unrestrained power'. The book concludes with a short Afterword in which I make the case for the reassertion of the values of liberty that are expressed in the Constitution, and for the renewal of the aspirations of the Founders.

The writing of this book has been, for me, a sobering as well as a most interesting experience. It has been salutary indeed to reflect upon how far the country has strayed from the vision of the Founders. I am very grateful to Harsh Mander for the stimulus to write this book, and for his perceptive comments on successive drafts. I am grateful, too, to Neera Chandhoke for her encouragement and her comments, and to my friends and colleagues of long standing—Stuart Corbridge, Chris Fuller, and Robin Jeffrey—for their careful criticism and helpful suggestions, to many of which—to my regret—I have been unable adequately to respond.

John Harriss
January 2024

# Chapter I

# A Very Short History of Liberty

## 'A Fancy, Modern Notion' and Its Ancient Origin

There is a famous depiction of 'Liberty' in European painting. This is in the picture of *Liberty Leading the People*, by the artist Eugene Delacroix, of 1831. Sometimes referred to as *Liberty on the barricades*, it shows a bare-breasted woman, waving the red, white and blue 'tricolour' flag of France in one hand, and bearing a musket in the other, leading a group of people over fallen bodies, with, in the background, what onlookers will recognize as the city of Paris, dominated by the cathedral of Notre Dame. On its tower there flies another tricolour, tiny in the painting. The people the woman leads are a varied lot. There is a man wearing a somewhat battered top hat, and with a neck-cloth still tied over his white shirt. He, too, brandishes a musket. There is a boy waving two pistols, and a young man who holds a sabre, with a pistol thrust into his trousers. Other figures are in the background, and indistinct, though we see swords waved above silhouetted heads. The man with the top hat is perhaps from the bourgeoisie, the boy a revolutionary worker, and the young man seems to be a student, wearing a type of hat associated with the French Revolution. The woman is Marianne, a portrayal of the Roman goddess of Liberty (*Libertas*), and the symbol to this day of the French Republic. She is also the inspiration for the calm figure of the Statue of Liberty, the gift of the people of France to the United States, that has for so long greeted travellers arriving in New York by sea. She is seen, too, as the personification of the slogan of the Revolution and later of the Republic, repeated on many public buildings to this day—*Liberté, Egalité, Fraternité*, or in English, liberty, equality and fraternity—words that appear also in the Preamble to the Constitution of India.

Often taken to be a depiction of the French Revolution of 1789, in fact Delacroix's painting commemorates another revolution in France, one that took place in 1830 to topple another monarch, Charles X. But the painting is rich in the symbolism of the Revolution of the late 18th century. The woman wears a red cap. It is a soft, conical cap that folds over at the top, of a kind associated with several peoples in different parts of the ancient world—called the Phrygian cap—and clearly depicted in their sculpture.

Though it was not, actually, the same as the felt cap that was worn by the emancipated slaves of Rome, it came to be seen in the 18th century as signifying freedom and the pursuit of liberty, first in the Netherlands, and then in both the French and the American Revolutions.

At the time of these great revolutions the idea of liberty was, according to one historian, among what were seen as 'fancy, modern notions'. But the symbolism of the Phrygian cap marks the lineage of the idea in Europe that is traced back to the world of Ancient Greece and Rome, in years before the beginning of the modern era. The *Digest* of Roman Law (530–533 CE) explained that 'the fundamental division of the law of persons is that all men and women are either free or are slaves'—the latter being the state of someone who, 'contrary to nature [is] subjected to the dominion of someone else'. A free subject, therefore, enjoying *libertas* (the Latin word for 'liberty' or 'freedom', as well as the name of the goddess), was someone who was *not* under such dominion. Until the 18th century, in Europe, liberty or 'freedom'—the two words can be treated as being synonymous with each other, as I go on to discuss—was generally understood as referring to the distinction made in Roman law between the slave and the free subject. It is a salutary reflection that if we understand the free subject as being someone not subjected to the dominion of another, then according to studies of Indian village society in the mid-20th century, at the time the Constitution was being written, many people weren't 'free' because they were subject to the 'dominion' of the leading landed families. This was true especially of those many Dalit labourers who were effectively tied in bondage to landlords. Even now, three-quarters of a century later, those in villages who, for example, don't own their own house sites (the case for quite large numbers), may be so heavily dependent on the landowners as to have their freedoms restricted. And as the great Roman statesman and philosopher, Cicero, argued, to enjoy liberty it is not enough to be free from coercion or the threat of it, it is necessary to be free from the *possibility* of being threatened or coerced. According to this argument, even the benevolent patron restricts the freedom of his clients. What takes away your liberty, in other words, is the simple fact of living at the mercy of someone else.

**Azaadi, 'Liberty' and 'Freedom'**

The English word 'liberty' has a number of meanings, but central among them are the ideas of 'freedom from arbitrary, despotic or autocratic control'—the classical idea, from the Latin, of not being subject to the dominion of another—and of 'independence, especially from a foreign power, monarchy or dictatorship'. These, for sure, were the ideas of those many Indians who struggled for freedom from colonial rule, often using the word *azaadi*, familiar to speakers of both Urdu and Hindi, which conveys the sense of having the right to make one's own decisions and of self-determination. In English these ideas are conveyed, as well, by the word 'freedom', which comes from Old German and means both 'the state of being able to act without hindrance or restraint' and—relatedly—'the state or fact of not being subject to despotic or autocratic control, or to a foreign power'.

These definitions, taken from the Oxford English Dictionary, show that 'liberty' and 'freedom' can be regarded, as I've said, as being synonymous, the one with the other. I want to argue, however, that the English word 'liberty' has come to have certain specific connotations, because of its association with the ideology of 'liberalism'. Liberalism was a very important influence in the thinking of many of those who drew up the Constitution of India—including some of the most influential among them. There was, though, always tension between liberal ideas, with their focus upon the rights of individuals, on the one hand, and the concern on the other for the transformation of society that was reflected very clearly, as I go on to argue, in the Resolution on Aims and Objects, introduced in the Constituent Assembly by Nehru, in December 1946, at the very beginning of the process of drawing up the Constitution. This may be seen as reflecting ideas of 'freedom', or *azaadi*, for Indian society, rather than the liberal focus on individual liberties.

**Liberty and Liberalism**

In 18th-century Europe the idea and the goal of realizing liberty were associated especially with the bourgeoisie. It was at this time that the system of ideas, or ideology, of liberalism became important. The word itself has the same Latin root as liberty—*liber*, an adjective meaning 'free'—and it refers to a broad body of ideas, centred on the importance of individual freedom. The standard Oxford English Dictionary, for instance, defines liberalism as 'Support for or advocacy of individual rights, civil liberties, and reform tending towards individual freedom, democracy or social equality; a political and social philosophy based on these beliefs'. The Dictionary finds the first use of 'liberalism' in English as late as 1816, in a report from Spain of accusations being made against those called the *Liberales*. These were the first politicians to claim the title of being 'liberal' and who, while not constituting a well-organized political party, shared opposition to the hereditary monarchy of Spain, and under whom there was a brief period of parliamentary rule after 1812. Liberalism was not then, and is not now a very precisely worked out political philosophy. As the historian Eric Hobsbawm once wrote, 'Its general assumptions about the world and man were marked by a pervasive individualism, which owed more to the introspection of middle class individuals or observation of their behaviour than to the principles on which it claimed to be based.' Liberal ideas and values were attractive to the increasingly significant bourgeoisies of Europe who sought freedom from the constraints to which they might be subjected by the monarchs who ruled over them, in order that they would be free to pursue their individual projects for bettering themselves in different ways.

Liberalism is an inheritance of the philosophy of the Enlightenment of 17th- and 18th-century Europe which was founded on the view that humanity is characterized above all by the capacity of reason, and that it is by means of the application of reason that we human beings can understand our universe and improve our own condition. The Enlightenment philosophers—Voltaire perhaps the most famous of them—took the view that it is essential always to challenge ideas and beliefs. Human minds should not be fettered in any way. The powers of reason must not be constrained. Thus the Enlightenment philosophers rejected the authority of the Church. Theirs was, we might say, a scientific viewpoint. They were protagonists, too, of the idea of progress—that through the use of reason, human beings can improve themselves and the societies in which they live. Human history is a story of ascent, not one—such as had been held by many medieval thinkers—of decline or stasis. The idea of progress finds a contemporary avatar in that of 'development', which postulates the possibility of improvement in our societies principally through increasing the productivity of the economy. Economic development, it is widely thought, is the necessary basis of broader social development and the improvement of individual lives.

Liberalism, then, very broadly, proposes that the world is made up by individuals who, possessing the faculty of reason and driven by various emotions, passions and interests, seek to maximize their own satisfactions—or happiness, as it was put in the American Declaration of Independence of 1776. The words of the Declaration of Independence point, though only by implication, to the recognition in the philosophy of liberalism that individuals' pursuit of their personal goals brings them into competition and conflict with others, who are doing the same thing. Social relationships between individuals cannot be avoided, and liberalism sees them, and the constitution of human societies, in terms of 'contract'. (The commercial terminology is another indication of the influence of middle-class experience in liberalism.) There is also the important idea of a 'social contract' between individual citizens and their rulers, or the governments of their societies—in which citizens consent, for example, to surrender some part of their income to the government, in exchange for its securing of their 'safety', or their well-being. Individual liberty—freedom from constraint—is necessarily limited by the exercise of their liberties by others. An absolutely crucial problem for government is that of managing the competition and conflict between individuals in such a way as to ensure that all are able to secure their 'satisfactions' to the extent possible, when all should have the same right to liberty.

Liberalism is distrustful of power, especially concentrated power (such as that of an imperial ruler, or of an autocratic demagogue), and it insists—in the face of power—on equal civic respect for the individual, and thus the importance of personal, political and property rights. Liberalism presupposes the freedom of the individual, subject to the necessary constraints of social life, and holds that property rights are necessary for the meaningful exercise of the other rights of the individual. Private property rights are foundational, too, in economic liberalism, the theory of which was set out by Adam Smith in *Wealth of Nations*, published in 1776. Smith showed how individuals' pursuit of their self-interest, in competition with one another, if left to operate as far as possible unchecked—so allowing for the 'hidden hand of the market'—could bring about rapid increase in the 'wealth of nations', and so of the 'happiness' of all. The increase in wealth comes about as a result of the activities of property-owning private enterprise, in the context of free markets and 'the liberal system of free exportation and free importation' (as Smith put it), making for the accumulation of capital. These ideas remain influential in contemporary economic thought, and these days it is taken as being more or less axiomatic that successful economies are based on private property ownership.

**Indian Liberalism**

Liberal ideas were profoundly influential in 19th- and early 20th-century India, and were engaged with, critically, by significant thinkers including Rammohan Roy and Dadabhai Naoroji, by politicians like Gokhale, as well as by many less well-known figures. Indian liberals sought the empowerment of their fellow countrymen with personal freedom, in the face of the despotism exercised by the British Raj. They tried, indeed, to use the ideas of great British liberal thinkers, like John Stuart Mill, against the imperial rulers. Purushottam Das Tandon reminded his listeners of this in the speech in which he seconded Nehru's presentation of the Resolution on Aims and Objects before the Constituent Assembly, in December 1946, when he said:

> We earnestly appealed to our rulers to treat us with justice. Our leaders referred them to their high ideals,

> to the ideals of Burke and Mill. They were steeped in British ideals and they hoped that the British would do them justice and give them freedom.

Tandon went on to say, however, that these appeals failed, and so 'drastic steps' of confrontation had to be taken in the course of the freedom struggle.

Indian liberals opposed, as well, traditional authority and what they saw as corrupt or morally wrong domestic and religious practices, such as child marriage. They wanted to improve society through education, perhaps particularly through the education of women. They sought representation in government service and on grand juries, and later in elective bodies. They were advocates of a free press and of the freedom of assembly. And though broadly supportive of individual property rights, they argued that these had to be subject to the need for protection of the masses against exploitation. They had a positive vision of liberty that was different, therefore, from that of their Western contemporaries, reflected in their concern, once they had secured office, for intervention by government to promote economic and social development in the interests of social justice. Indian liberalism departed from that of Britain because Indian liberals placed much less emphasis on individualism, and were sympathetic to ideas about the importance of community in people's lives. The historian Christopher Bayly has argued:

> Liberalism was a broad field on which Indians and other South Asians began not only to resist colonial rule but to engage in debates about the Good Life as would-be citizens ... [rather than colonial subjects]. Their ideas, even when rejected, or transformed out of recognition by their political successors and enemies, were...foundational to all forms of Indian nationalism and the country's modern politics[.]

With this remark, Bayly refers to the way in which, by the middle of the 20th century, liberalism had come to be regarded very critically in India, as it was by the historian and diplomat, K.M. Panikkar. He argued in his book, *The State and the Citizen*, that Indians had always been suspicious of the British liberal tradition because it so easily masked oppression. He referred to classical Indian ideas in which the state was seen as being responsible not just for securing order, but for protecting *dharma* and righteousness (connoting social justice). Many of the members of the Constituent Assembly that was responsible for drawing up the Constitution of India were uncomfortable with the extent to which it drew on Western liberal precedents, such as the American Constitution, and expressed regret that it did not draw much more on distinctively Indian concepts and historical practices. Even such central figures as Nehru and Dr Ambedkar either ignored or were explicitly critical of some of the tenets of liberalism. And yet, in its language—beginning with the Preamble, and its explicit reference to the slogan of the French Revolution—and in its essential features, the Constitution of India reflects liberal constitutional values. These are evident in such features of the Constitution as the recognition of rights—including the right of personal liberty, the power of judicial review and the principle of the separation of powers between the executive, the legislature and the judiciary.

### 'Hardly Arrived in the Mail, From Overseas': Ideas in the Constitution of India

It was perhaps both a strength and a weakness of India's political elite of the mid-20th century—the elite that drew up the Constitution and determined the initial path of the new republic—that its members drew on different traditions of Western political thought, and to some extent on classical Indian political thinking. The second major tradition of Western political thought that influenced some members of this elite—including Nehru and Ambedkar—was socialism, which breaks away radically from the liberal assumption that society is constituted by rational individuals, pursuing their own self-interest, in competition with one another. Socialism reasserts the idea that human beings are communal creatures, living together and supporting each other. A condition for such shared human life is individual freedom, but this is to be realized through overcoming class exploitation. As George Bernard Shaw said, in writing on 'Socialism and Liberty', people are subjected to tyrannies, 'because the people who can refuse us employment or the use of land have powers of life and death over us, and can make us do what they like, law or no law'. For this reason one of the major principles of socialism is that there should be common, social ownership of the means of production, not private property. Some members of the Constituent Assembly, including Dr Ambedkar, at the outset, advocated the nationalization of industry and of land, in the interests of securing for the people justice and equality, and liberty.

I've said that the fact that the members of the political elite, including those who came together in the Constituent Assembly, drew on different and in some ways, certainly, opposing political ideas, was both a strength and a weakness. It was a strength in that they generally sought to address the specific conditions and needs of India and were not just following a model taken from elsewhere—as one scholar has put it, the Constitution 'hardly arrived in the mail, from overseas'. It was a weakness, however, in that it led to what was an awkward, and ultimately unsuccessful combination of liberal democracy and a version of Soviet central planning. The awkwardness was expressed, unwittingly perhaps, in Nehru's speech to introduce the Resolution on Aims and Objects, on 13 December 1946, when he sought to anticipate the criticism that the Resolution did not say that India should be a socialist state. He went on:

> I stand for Socialism and, I hope, India will stand for Socialism and that India will go towards the constitution of a Socialist State and I do believe that the whole world will have to go that way. What form of Socialism again is another matter for your considerations. But the main thing is that in such a Resolution, if, in accordance with my own desire, I had put in, that we want a Socialist State, we would have put in something which may be agreeable to many and may not be agreeable to some and we wanted this Resolution not to be controversial in regard to such matters.

There were uneasy and difficult compromises made in the Constituent Assembly—which proceeded by consensus, not by majority voting—over private property, as well as over the conditions that should or should not be applied to individual liberties, and how far the state should be legally required to satisfy the demands of social justice.

In their concern for social justice, Indian liberals, and the Constituent Assembly, largely followed John Stuart Mill in recognizing and working with the distinction between liberty understood as *absence of coercion*, and liberty as *freedom to act.* The distinction is sometimes understood as being between negative and positive liberty, or between *freedom from* and *freedom to.* Thus, in the freedom struggle, Indians sought freedom from oppressive, arbitrary and despotic colonial rule and, some of them more than others, freedom from the oppression of tradition in their own society, including the oppression of caste. They sought, in other words, 'absence of coercion'. These are negative freedoms. They also espoused, much more vigorously, certainly than 19th-century British liberals, the positive freedoms that follow from their government's ensuring that citizens have a decent standard of living (a standard of living that means that they can live with dignity and independence), and the education and good health that is necessary for them to develop their capacities as human beings. This is what Jawaharlal Nehru promised in the wonderful, compelling words—reflecting his particular way of bringing together liberal and socialist ideas—with which he summed up in the debate on the Resolution on Aims and Objects, on 22 January 1947:

> The first task of this Assembly is to free India through a new constitution, to feed the starving people and [clothe] the naked masses and to give every Indian fullest opportunity to develop himself according to his capacity.

He went on later in his speech:

> I trust the Constitution itself will lead us into the real freedom we have clamoured for, and that real freedom, in turn, will bring food to our starving peoples, clothing for them, housing for them, and all manner of opportunities of progress.

So 'real freedom', for Nehru, and for most of the members of the Constituent Assembly, meant something different, and—it may be argued—something *more* than the negative individual freedoms that are at the heart of liberalism. 'Freedom not as an appurtenance of privilege... but as a prescriptive right extending...into the intimate organization of society', as the great radical thinker, Karl Polanyi, put it in his book *The Great Transformation*, published in 1944.

**Liberty in Doubt**

The historian of the Constitution, Granville Austin, described it as a 'seamless web', in which three strands are woven together, being mutually dependent and essentially intertwined: establishing democracy; protecting and enhancing national unity and integrity; and fostering the social transformation that Nehru spoke about so eloquently in the speech from which I have just quoted. These strands are woven together in the Constitution, no doubt. Certainly that was the intention of the Founders, as we may describe the leaders of the freedom struggle, and the members of the Constituent Assembly. For all that, there were profound disagreements among them—as Nehru recognized when he introduced the Resolution on Aims and Objects. But weaknesses in the web soon became apparent as the Constitution was put to work in independent India.

This book is concerned with the tensions between the civil and political liberties that are essential in a democracy, and the demands both of social transformation and of the protection of national unity and integrity. It has been above all the latter—the demands of unity and integrity—that have put the liberties that were said by members of the Constituent Assembly to be the heart of the Constitution to severe test. We should remember that the Constitution was drawn up amid conditions of insccurity, when the integrity of the nation was under threat. These were the years of Partition and of the communal violence associated with it; of the assassination of Gandhi; of the struggle in and over Kashmir; of struggles in the Northeast and of the communist-led peasant insurgency in Telangana. They were years, too, in which anti-colonial struggles continued elsewhere in Asia—in Indonesia and Indochina—and Western intervention remained a constant threat. It is hardly surprising that the great majority of the Founders believed that there must be a strong central government, or that they should have conceded the need for individual liberty to be limited by the needs of national security. It is hardly surprising that they should have consented, therefore, to retaining with little modification, a good many of the repressive laws of the colonial state. The Preventive Detention Act, in the vein of a long sequence of colonial laws and unquestionably a danger to liberty, was passed by Parliament just thirty days after the Constitution came into force.

# Chapter II

# Liberty

## The Pledges of the Constitution of India

Liberty was what the struggle for independence was all about, and from an early stage in the struggle, its leaders recognized that freedom *from* the coercion of imperial rule must bring, as well, the positive freedoms (the freedoms *to*) that Nehru was referring to in the speech from which I quoted towards the end of the last chapter. In the end, in the Constitution, negative and positive freedoms are set out in the Fundamental Rights of Part III and the Directive Principles of Part IV. These were, according to members of the Constituent Assembly, the heart of the Constitution, and they 'had their roots deep in the struggle for independence' (the words of Granville Austin). The Fundamental Rights are, in general, statements of the negative obligations of the state not to encroach upon individual liberty that have been well established since the French and American revolutions of the 18th century; most of the Directive Principles aim at making Indians free in the positive sense, so that they should be able to lead lives that they have reason to value. Together, the Fundamental Rights and the Directive Principles were intended to ensure that liberty should no longer be the privilege of only a few people in Indian society.

**Forerunners**

Many of the Articles concerning the Fundamental Rights first appeared in the Report of the Motilal Nehru Committee in 1928. Both this document, and the subsequent Karachi Resolution of the Congress, of 1931, were in many ways more radical than the Constitution, and bolder in their departures from the liberal conception of liberty.

The Motilal Nehru Committee was set up in the context of the appointment by the British government, late in 1927, of the Simon Commission, entrusted with the task of proposing constitutional reforms for India. The fact that the Commission included not a single Indian member had brought an angry response from the leaders of the nationalist movement, but then the reply of the British was to challenge Indians to show that they could design a constitution for themselves. This was the task taken up by the Committee chaired by Motilal Nehru—whose son Jawaharlal was appointed the secretary—and the Committee's Report was written in the form of a constitutional document. In an editorial, the *Hindustan Times* said of it, 'we have drawn up the Magna Carta of our liberty' (referring to the charter that is usually taken as the foundation stone of democracy in Britain).

The 'Fundamental Rights' section of the Report substantially anticipates that in the Constitution of 1950, with ten of its 19 sub-clauses re-appearing in the later document, largely unchanged. Where the Report differs quite significantly from the Constitution of 1950 is by including among the 'fundamental rights', certain economic and social rights that were included only among the less binding Directive Principles. Thus sub-clause five stated 'All citizens in the Commonwealth of India have the right to free elementary education...and such right shall be enforceable as soon as due arrangements shall have been made by competent authority'; whereas the Constitution of 1950 included this provision among the Directive Principles, Article 45: 'The state shall endeavour to provide, within a period of ten years from the commencement of the Constitution, for free and compulsory education for all children until they complete the age of fourteen years'. The proposal in the Motilal Nehru Report that citizens should have 'the right to free elementary education' is a good deal more forceful than the language of the Constitution, about the state's 'endeavouring' to provide such education. Then in sub-clause 17 the Report said 'Parliament shall make suitable laws for the maintenance of health and fitness for work of all citizens, securing of a living wage for every worker, the protection of motherhood, welfare of children, and the economic consequences of old age, infirmity and unemployment', the elements of which re-appeared among the Directive Principles ('improving public health', in Article 47; 'securing of a living wage', in Article 43; 'protection of motherhood' as 'maternity benefit', in Article 42; 'welfare of children', in Article 39, though only after the 42nd Amendment of 1976; and 'economic consequences of old age [etc.]', in Article 41, with its reference to 'undeserved want'). It is notable that the Report was sometimes more specific than the Constitution, as it was also in sub-clause 15 which stated, 'Freedom of combination and association for the maintenance and improvement of labour and economic conditions is guaranteed to everyone and of all occupations.' The provisions included in the Nehru Report concerning these social and economic rights were radical at the time of their formulation and showed how far Indian liberals had moved beyond most of their peers in Britain.

The commitments of the Nehru Report were repeated in the Karachi Resolution passed by the Indian National

Congress at its 1931 session. The first paragraph of the Resolution stated, 'This Congress is of the opinion that in order to end the exploitation of the masses, political freedom must include real economic freedom of the starving millions...'—an earlier expression of the ideas contained in Nehru's concluding address in the debate on the Resolution on Aims and Objects. The document went on to specify the requirements of such economic freedom, as well as re-stating, in paragraph two, the fundamental rights that protect civil liberties. The Resolution lists socio-economic principles—making for positive freedoms—that the Indian state should adhere to: 'A living wage for industrial workers, limited hours of labour, healthy conditions of work, protection against the economic consequences of old age, sickness and unemployment'; 'Labour to be freed from serfdom...'; 'Protection of women workers...provisions for leave during maternity period'; 'Prohibition of employment of children of school going age in factories'; 'Right of labour to form unions...'; 'Free primary education'. All of this presupposed more intervention by the state than many liberals were (and some still are) comfortable with.

Where the Karachi Resolution differed from the Nehru Report was in regard to property. The Report reflected the influence of liberal ideas, among which—as I pointed out in chapter one—the right to property is linked with life and liberty. The second clause of the paragraph listing fundamental rights reads: 'No person shall be deprived of his liberty, nor shall his dwelling or property be entered, sequestered or confiscated, save in accordance with law. All titles to private and personal property lawfully acquired... are hereby guaranteed.' The Karachi Resolution, however, reflecting the stronger influence of socialist ideas, does not include the right to property among 'the fundamental rights of the people', and promises both 'Substantial reduction of land revenue and rent...' and 'Control by the state of key industries and mineral resources'. The question of rights to property was one that was to figure prominently in the early years of the Indian Republic after 1950, as I will go on to discuss in the next chapters.

What were finally agreed to and included as the fundamental rights—including the right to property—and the directive principles in the Constitution of India had to an important extent, therefore, already been elaborated and discussed even before the Constituent Assembly, the members of which had been elected on a franchise restricted to about 20 per cent of the possible electorate, first met.

## Aims and Objects

The Resolution on Aims and Objects that was placed before the Constituent Assembly by Jawaharlal Nehru on 13 December 1946 began with the words 'This Constituent Assembly declares its firm and solemn resolve to proclaim India as an Independent, Sovereign Republic, and to draw up for her future governance a Constitution', and, it went on in the fifth clause, 'WHEREIN shall be guaranteed and secured to all the people of India justice, social, economic and political; equality of status, of opportunity and before the law; freedom of thought, expression, belief, faith, worship, vocation, association and action, subject to law and public morality'. Nehru went on to speak of this as a pledge, to the present and the future people of India. It is noteworthy that the Resolution has no specific reference to liberty, though it lists basic freedoms, and emphasizes the intention to secure justice, in its several dimensions.

The pledge of the fifth clause was effectively repeated in the Preamble to the Constitution, though with the addition of specific references to liberty and fraternity. The Preamble—quoted in the prologue to this book—speaks of the 'solemn resolve' to secure to all the citizens of the Republic of India, JUSTICE, LIBERTY, EQUALITY and to promote among them all FRATERNITY. As Dr Ambedkar—as the chairman of the Drafting Committee—observed, in his great final speech before the Constituent Assembly, on 25 November 1949, these values are all inherently related to one another. He said:

> These principles of liberty, equality and fraternity are not to be treated as separate items in a trinity. They form a union of trinity in the sense that to divorce one from the other is to defeat the very purpose of democracy. Liberty cannot be divorced from equality, equality cannot be divorced from liberty. Nor can liberty and equality be divorced from fraternity. Without equality, liberty would produce the supremacy of the few over the many. Equality without liberty would kill individual initiative. Without fraternity, liberty [and] equality could not become a natural course of things.

Fraternity meant for Ambedkar 'a sense of common brotherhood for all Indians', set against all forms of discrimination. In a brilliant article on the subject, Harsh Mander similarly argues that it means 'a sense of mutual belonging and respect that transcends all other differences between people'. For both, then, fraternity is a necessary corollary of liberty and equality. And though Ambedkar didn't say so in this speech, it is also evident that justice, or fairness—'social, economic and political'—which is also part of the pledge of the Preamble, is unimaginable in the absence of liberty, equality and fraternity.

What Ambedkar also didn't say at this point is that the values of liberty and equality are, to some extent, also in conflict with one another, and that it is very important to establish a balance between them. In the United States, for instance, as the Chinese scholar (and senior member of the Politburo Standing Committee of the Chinese Communist Party) Wang Huning noted, there is a contradiction between Americans' supposed desire for equality and their fixation with freedom. A fixation with freedom is reflected in the appeal that Donald Trump makes to many Americans. In the end, liberty or freedom trumps all else, often leading to the worst effects of individualism. A member of the Constituent Assembly, Professor K.T. Shah, one of the more prolific participants in the debates, whose contributions, though they rarely persuaded the House, were acknowledged by Ambedkar, recognized this problem. He argued that if social justice was to be secured then individuals must recognize their obligations to others. In responding to Ambedkar's initial presentation of the Draft Constitution, on 5 November 1948, he said:

> [W]e are living in an age when we think so much of freedom; and talk in terms of individual liberty so much that we are apt to forget that 'freedom' is likely to degenerate into 'license' if we do not care to remember the need simultaneously for self-discipline [and] that freedom has its obligations just as much as its advantages.

The wisdom of Shah's remark was shown very clearly in the context of the coronavirus pandemic when there were many people, in some countries more than others, who refused to respect their obligations to others, valuing above all their individual freedom and their right, for example, not to use a mask, to respect the need for social distancing, or to be vaccinated.

In tension with each other but inherently related to one another though the values of the Constitution are, there is a sense in which liberty is foundational. Liberty, in the limited sense of freedom from colonial rule—a specific instance of the core meaning of 'liberty' as 'freedom from arbitrary, despotic or autocratic rule'—was what the long struggle for independence was all about. Then, in the Constitution, the Founders aimed to specify what 'freedom' must mean beyond just 'independence', and in doing so to show how it should be secured. The Constitution was to be, in the words of one member of the Assembly, 'a charter of liberty',* and as such Part III of the Constitution, on the Fundamental Rights, and Part IV, on the Directive Principles of State Policy—though their articles may account, between them, for only about one tenth of the total—are its heart.

## Right to Freedom

Freedom, as I've suggested in chapter one of this book, and in this one, can be thought of as having negative

* Sardar Ujjal Singh, 17 December 1946.

and positive aspects. Negative freedoms include essentially freedom *from* arbitrary, despotic control, or in more immediate terms, freedom from detention—being deprived of liberty—without legally justified cause and without the right of fair trial, freedom from torture, and the right to life itself. In the Constitution of India these freedoms are provided for in Article 20, which refers to 'Protection in respect of conviction for offences', in Article 21—'Protection of life and liberty', and in the problematic Article 22—'Protection against arrest and detention in certain cases'. The last was said to have been 'ironically located in the chapter on fundamental rights'—and as I said in the Preface, I find it a kind of a Trojan Horse, letting the executive in, and in such a way as to enable it to abrogate freedoms, avoiding judicial scrutiny. Although originally introduced by Dr Ambedkar with the intention of providing safeguards against misuse of police powers of the state to make arrests and detentions, a late amendment to it excluded preventive detention cases (in which people are arrested before they commit an offence, and without trial, on the grounds of suspicion alone) from direct judicial scrutiny.

The second of the articles, Article 21, includes few words—'No person shall be deprived of his life or personal liberty except according to procedure established by law'—but it is the crucial one, and it prompted substantial debate in the Assembly, having to do essentially with its wording and what the words used implied with regard to the powers of parliament on the one hand, and those of the judiciary on the other. I'll discuss this, and the problems of Article 22, in the next chapter. The controversy over it notwithstanding, Article 21, together with Article 19 in the section of the Constitution (in Part III) that has the title 'Right to Freedom', may be held, as they were by members of the Constituent Assembly, to constitute 'the charter of our liberties'.

Article 19 refers to vitally important positive freedoms (freedoms *to*). It concerns 'Protection of certain rights regarding freedom of speech, etc.', and under its first sub-clause it specifies that:

> All citizens shall have the right—
> to freedom of speech and expression;
> to assemble peaceably and without arms;
> to form associations or unions or cooperative societies;
> to move freely throughout the territory of India;
> to acquire, hold or dispose of property [sub-clause deleted by the 44th Amendment of 1978];
> to reside and settle in any part of the territory of India; and
> to practise any profession, or to carry on any occupation, trade or business.

The further clauses under Article 19, however, proceed to specify a range of conditions that apply to the exercise of these freedoms, and some members of the Constituent Assembly argued that these would have the effect of taking away the freedoms in practice. This was the second principal controversy over the Fundamental Rights, and over liberty, that was engaged during the debates over the Draft Constitution. This, too, is discussed in the next chapter.

The positive freedoms—freedoms to act in significant ways—are extended to religion in Article 25 which specifies 'Freedom of conscience and free profession, practice and propagation of religion', and is itself then extended in Articles 26 to 28, concerning the management of religious affairs, taxation by religious bodies, and religious instruction. In all cases individual citizens are to be free to make their own decisions.

Others of the Fundamental Rights specified in the Constitution also set out negative freedoms. Article 15 concerns the 'Prohibition of discrimination on grounds of religion, race, caste, sex, or place of birth', and Article 17, 'Abolition of Untouchability'. Of course, there are political regimes in which discrimination is legally embedded. The most notorious of them was the apartheid regime that prevailed in the Republic of South Africa which denied Black South Africans of rights of citizenship such as those that are laid out in Article 19 of the Constitution of India. Now, very sadly, much the same is true of Arabs in the state of Israel. Discrimination on grounds of religion, race, caste, sex or place of birth has not been legally established in India, until very recently. Now—as I'll discuss in chapter five—fundamental freedoms of large numbers of Indians *are* being threatened on grounds of religion and in some cases those of place of birth. Historically, too, and still in the present, in spite of Article 17 of the Constitution, the freedoms of many Indians are constrained by the social practices associated with caste that have nothing to do with the state. As the Tamil writer Perumal Murugan wrote in an essay in 2021, 'In Indian society freedom is hostage to the caste system. The space that each caste can inhabit and traverse is clearly demarcated. It is impossible to step out of that space and enter another.' Dalits and Adivasis still experience discrimination in all sorts of ways, whether, for instance, in the treatment to which they may be subjected when they approach local officials, or in their continuing exclusion from some public places, or in their access to employment. They don't, in practice, enjoy the same rights—the same liberty—as others among their fellow citizens.

Discrimination in employment connects up with another of the negative freedoms that are set out in the Fundamental Rights—in Article 23, concerning 'Prohibition of traffic in human beings and forced labour'. While practices of forced labour such, notably, as *begar*—

rendering service to a 'master' without payment at all, or for very minimal pay, which was of great concern to members of the Constituent Assembly—may be less prevalent than they were in the mid-20th century and before, there remain elements of forced labour in the employment relations into which many Indians are effectively compelled, by poverty, to enter. Very many of them are Dalits or Adivasis. These are other matters that I will discuss further later in the book.

**Freedom From Want—the Directive Principles**

The Fundamental Rights, therefore, establish three of the four freedoms that US President Franklin D. Roosevelt laid out in his State of the Union Address in 1941. Article 21, in particular, together with other articles including 17, 19 and 23, should make for 'freedom from fear'; Article 19 specifically establishes the right to 'freedom of speech'; Article 25 specifies 'freedom of worship'. But what of Roosevelt's fourth freedom—'freedom from want'? Or if we think back to Nehru's statement about the purpose of securing freedom when he closed the debate on Aims and Objects, and spoke of ensuring that Indians are properly fed and clothed and enabled to develop themselves according to their capacities, where does the Constitution lay out these positive freedoms? The Fundamental Rights of the Constitution really don't establish freedom from want, or the positive freedoms of which Nehru spoke—except in the right to life of Article 21 in the way in which it has been interpreted in recent years by judges of the Supreme Court (as I will discuss in chapter four). Freedom from want, and the positive freedoms associated with it—which should make it possible for all Indians to be able to lead lives that they have reason to value—are not established in the Fundamental Rights for the reason set out very clearly by the great civil servant who advised the Constituent Assembly, B.N. Rau (later India's representative on the Security Council of the United Nations), in his 'Preliminary Notes on Fundamental Rights', written in 1946. There he said:

> [I]t is useful to recognise a distinction between two broad classes of rights: there are certain rights that require positive action by the State and which can be guaranteed only so far as such action is practicable, while others merely require that the State shall abstain from prejudicial action. Typical of the former is the right to work, which cannot be guaranteed further than by requiring the State, [in] the language of the Irish Constitution 'to direct its policy towards securing that the citizens may, through their occupations, find the means of making reasonable provision for their domestic needs'; typical of the latter is the right which requires, in the language of the American Constitution, that 'the State shall not deprive any citizen of his liberty

> without due process of law'. *It is obvious that rights of the first type are not normally either capable of, or suitable for, enforcement by legal action*, while those of the second type may be so enforced. (Emphasis added)

I have highlighted Rau's words about it being obvious that 'rights that require positive action by the State' are not usually capable of or suitable for 'enforcement by legal action', because this was a view that was fiercely contested by some members of the Constituent Assembly. The rights that Rau was talking about are economic and social rights—like the right to work to which he referred—as opposed to what are usually described as civil and political rights such as the right to life and liberty, and the rights set out in detail in Article 19 of the Constitution, about rights to freedom of expression, assembly, association, movement, residence and vocation. The right to vote is another such 'liberty', and that it was not explicitly included in the Fundamental Rights worried some members of the Constituent Assembly. With regard to economic and social rights Rau argued that it was just not practicable for the state to provide legally-binding (or in other words, justiciable) guarantees, and his argument was accepted in the Interim Report on Fundamental Rights that was presented to the Constituent Assembly on 29 April 1947 by Sardar Patel, as the chairman of the Advisory Committee on the Subject of Fundamental Rights. Patel reported in his brief introduction that the committee had 'come to the conclusion that the fundamental rights should be divided into two parts, the first part justiciable and the other part non-justiciable'. The Interim Report was concerned only with those rights that it was thought should be justiciable.

A year and a half later, on 4 November 1948, Dr Ambedkar introduced the Draft Constitution to the Assembly, and it was then that the Directive Principles of State Policy, set out in Part IV—the second, non-justiciable part of the fundamental rights—first came up for discussion. It is in the Directive Principles that we find the provisions of the Constitution for freedom from want, and in the words, again, of Granville Austin, they 'set forth the humanitarian socialist precepts that were the aims of the Indian social revolution'. As Ambedkar explained, the Directive Principles were a novel feature of the Constitution—at that time only the Constitution of the Irish Free State made similar provisions—and he described them as 'instructions' to future governments. Whoever captures state power in future, he said, will not be free to do whatever they like with this power, because they will be bound, by the Constitution, to aim to realize the principles that were set out. This is what is explained in Article 37, which reads:

> The provisions contained in this part [Part IV] shall not be enforceable by any court, but the principles

> therein laid down are nonetheless fundamental in the governance of the country and it shall be the duty of the State to apply these principles in making laws.

Ambedkar necessarily admitted that the Directive Principles had no legal force behind them, but—anticipating the criticism that he knew would follow from some members of the Assembly—he went on, 'I am not prepared to admit that they have no sort of binding force at all. Nor am I prepared to concede that they are useless because they have no binding force in law.' As he argued later, it was not for the Constitution to lay down government policy, such as some members of the Assembly wished for when they said that the Constitution should specify that independent India would be socialist. This, indeed, seemed to be what Ambedkar himself had wished for at the outset of the deliberations of the Constituent Assembly. But he evidently saw the need, in a democracy, to respect different views of what state policy should be. The Directive Principles were a kind of a compromise, defining the aims that all governments should set out to achieve, without actually laying down specific policies. The Directive Principles together amount to instructions to the State, exactly as Ambedkar said, to aim to bring about the fundamental transformation of Indian society through the following measures, in the main:

1. Securing 'social order for promotion of the welfare of the people', and minimizing inequalities between individuals and groups (Article 38)
2. Providing for 'adequate means of livelihood' for all; making sure that the material resources of the country are owned and controlled in such a way as to serve 'the common good'; ensuring that the economy works in such a way as not to result in concentration of wealth and ownership of the means of production 'to the common detriment'; ensuring that there is equal pay for equal work for both men and women; ensuring that no citizens should be forced to take up jobs to which they aren't suited because of their age or strength; and (thanks to the 42nd Amendment of 1976) protecting children (Article 39)
3. Making 'effective provision', 'within the limits of [the State's] economic capacity and development', for the right to work, the right to education, and the right to public assistance (in cases of 'undeserved want') (Article 41)
4. Ensuring 'just and humane conditions of work', and maternity relief (Article 42)
5. Endeavouring to ensure that all workers receive a living wage and conditions of work so as to be able to have 'a decent standard of life and

full enjoyment of leisure and social and cultural opportunities' (Article 43)

6. Endeavouring 'to provide, within a period of ten years from the commencement of the Constitution, for free and compulsory education [to children] until they complete the age of fourteen years' (Article 45; replaced in the 86th Amendment, when basic education became a fundamental right under the new Article 21A, by a commitment to providing 'early childhood care and education for all children until they complete the age of six')
7. Promoting the educational and economic interests of Scheduled Castes, Scheduled Tribes and other 'weaker sections' of the people (Article 46)
8. Raising the level of nutrition and the standard of living of the people, and improving public health (regarded as being 'among primary duties' of the State) (Article 47)

In all cases, the wording of the Constitution means that the state should be *trying* to do all these things, while recognizing, as in Article 41, that it will be constrained by 'the limits of its economic capacity and development'. There are other provisions among the Directive Principles, including Article 40, concerning the 'Organization of village panchayats', and a few additions that have been provided for by amendments that add directly to the agenda of social transformation, including the amendment of Article 45 concerning early childhood care. But the essentials are contained in the points that I have listed. Together they constitute an agenda for achieving for all Indian citizens the *freedom to* live lives they have reason to value, so realizing the great objective that Nehru set out in closing the debate on the Resolution on Aims and Objects when he spoke of every Indian having not only adequate food and clothing but also 'the fullest opportunity to develop himself according to his capacity'.

It is an agenda for social democracy, rather than for socialism—if by the latter term we mean an economic system based on common ownership rather than on private property. Many of the Founders professed a commitment to socialism, but there was certainly not a majority in favour of common ownership, and the Fundamental Rights originally included, in Article 19, the right of individuals 'to acquire, hold or dispose of property' (removed by the 44th Amendment in 1978). When Dr Ambedkar responded to Nehru's proposal of the Resolution on Aims and Objects in December 1946, he said that he found it 'somewhat disappointing', because he thought that if the aim really was to achieve economic, social and political justice, then the Resolution should have stated 'in most explicit terms that in order that there may be social and economic justice in the country there would be nationalization of industry and nationalization of land'. Neither then, however, nor at any other time did he explicitly state a commitment to nationalization, and when he presented the final draft of the Constitution in November 1949, he used the words 'social democracy'. He said, 'We must make our political democracy a social democracy as well. Political democracy cannot last unless there lies at the base of it social democracy.' In a functioning social democracy capitalism is regulated in the interests of social justice—and this is what is sought in the Directive Principles of State Policy.

In his statement about political democracy needing to be based in social democracy Ambedkar showed remarkable foresight. Now, three-quarters of a century later, it is being argued by noted thinkers that the reason why democracy is very widely in retreat is ultimately because of the 'market-friendly' or neoliberal economic policies that have been pursued across the world, including in India, over the last forty years—what is sometimes described as 'laissez-faire' policy. These French words imply that states should intervene very little in the economy—really the opposite of what is proposed through the Directive Principles. 'Market-friendly' policies have had the effect, very widely, of making livelihoods precarious. One of the thinkers I have in mind, Martin Wolf, for long the chief economics correspondent of the London-based *Financial Times,* wrote very recently, 'The insecurity that laissez-faire generates for the great majority...is ultimately incompatible with democracy'. The Indian economist, Pranab Bardhan, argues in the same way in a book called *A World of Insecurity*, in which he shows how these economic policies have created conditions not only of acute economic insecurity, but also of cultural insecurity for very many people. Insecurity, in turn, has led lots of people to be persuaded by 'strongman' political leaders who promise to change things, commonly by 'making the country great again', and who use the power that they achieve through these appeals to trample upon democracy, and often to abuse freedoms like those set out in Article 19, or by detaining critics without trial. Bardhan argues that the best way to counter such demagogues is to rejuvenate social democracy—to regulate capitalism, in other words, in such a way as to bring about economic and social justice. This is precisely what Ambedkar was driving at when he said that '[w]e must make our political democracy a social democracy as well'. Political democracy depends on the striving for 'justice, social, economic and political' and it requires that the state must intervene in the operation of the economy so that it works in the interests of justice, exactly as is proposed in Articles 38 and 39 of the Constitution.

# Chapter III

# A Glass Half Empty?

## Contestation Over Liberties

### Liberty Challenged

The sixteenth Chief Justice of India, Yeshwant Vishnu Chandrachud, once wrote of Articles 14, 19 and 21 of the Constitution as a 'golden triangle', standing 'between the heaven of freedom into which Tagore wanted his country to awake and the abyss of unrestrained power'. Article 14 refers to 'Equality before law—The State shall not deny to any person equality before the law or the equal protection of the laws within the territory of India'. This article, originally included in the Draft Constitution of 1948 within what was eventually to become Article 21, has never been controversial. Both the other two articles in the 'golden triangle' have, however, been the cause of considerable controversy, in the Constituent Assembly and in the subsequent deliberations of Parliament and of the judiciary. The controversies over the right to freedom of speech and expression, the right to property, and over preventive detention and restriction of the right to liberty have all led to confrontations between the legislature and the judiciary.

It is important to remember that the period of the drafting of the Constitution and then of its initial implementation was a time in which the Indian state was subject to significant security threats, with communal violence across North India over Partition, war with Pakistan in Kashmir, and armed insurgencies going on in several parts of the country, most importantly in Telangana. It is ironic that freedom in India, once achieved, was soon subjected to challenges from the demands both of social transformation—which is what the controversies over private property were about—and of the quest for security and national unity. The 'seamless web' of the Constitution, as Granville Austin described it, soon began to be stretched.

In this chapter I first consider the arguments in the Constituent Assembly about the drafts of what became Articles 19 and 21, and then examine what happened to them over the years after 1950. I'll refer, as well, to the severe limitations on liberty over long periods in some parts of India. A simple conclusion is that the history of civil liberties betrays an authoritarian tendency on the part of successive governments of India, so skirting, at best, the 'abyss of unrestrained power'. In chapter five I'll carry the story into the present century, and the era of the majoritarian government of the BJP. I'll ask, as well, what we learn of liberty in the daily lives of Indian citizens from the studies of sociologists and others, in a short *intermezzo*, between this chapter and the one which follows it, on the fate of social and economic rights such as provide for positive freedoms.

I'll not discuss here other articles of the Constitution that are intended to guarantee important freedoms—Articles 15 (on discrimination), 17 (on untouchability), 23 (on forced labour), and especially 25, concerned with freedom of conscience and worship (the fourth freedom in President Roosevelt's list). This is not because these articles aren't important. They certainly are, but they were not the objects of much controversy in the Constituent Assembly, save for differences over the right to propagate religion in Article 25. Apart from Article 15—subject to amendments intended to allow the state to provide positive discrimination for historically marginalized and oppressed communities—these articles have not been contested until the more recent past. I refer to them, therefore, in the Intermezzo before chapter four, and again in chapter five.

## Civil Liberties in the Constituent Assembly Debates

Article 19 (as it became) won very strong support in the Constituent Assembly. Kazi Syed Karimuddin, a lawyer and a member of the Assembly from the Muslim League called 'this article...the very life of the Draft Constitution'; Professor Shibban Lal Saxena, a freedom fighter with a background in the labour movement, put it eloquently when he said 'this article may be truly stated to be the charter of our liberties'.* Yet it also occasioned considerable controversy. When he introduced the Draft Constitution, on 4 November 1948, Dr Ambedkar referred to the fact that 'the most criticized part...is that which relates to the Fundamental Rights'—and as the transcript of the Assembly debates shows, much of the controversy had to do with the provisos, or conditions, that were attached to the freedoms specified in Article 19. The big question was that of how far fundamental rights should be subject to limitation.

Article 21 (Article 15, as it was in the Draft Constitution) was linked with Article 19 (Article 13 in the Draft) as 'the bedrock of our liberties', but was the object of considerable unease over its wording. There was fierce debate over whether the article should state—as was finally agreed—that the right to life and personal liberty is subject 'to procedure established by law' rather than to

* Interventions of 2 December 1948.

'due process of law', which was the language used in the Interim Report on Fundamental Rights. The point at issue here, as in other parts of the debates in the Constituent Assembly, had to do with 'the question of the relationship between the legislature and the judiciary', as Ambedkar said in his response to proposed amendments (on 13 December 1948). How far should the powers of the judiciary to check legislation passed by a democratically elected legislature extend?

### *Article 19*

The Interim Report on Fundamental Rights, presented to the Assembly by Sardar Patel in April 1947, and generally received very favourably, made all the liberties of Article 19 (freedoms of speech, assembly, association, residence, movement and vocation) 'subject to public order and morality or to the existence of grave emergency declared to be such by the government of the Union'. Then other, more specific conditions were applied to each of the liberties. In response, a number of speakers argued that the various provisos attached to each right, in the words of Somnath Lahiri, the sole member of the Assembly from the Communist Party of India, 'tak[e] away the right almost completely'.* He pointed out, too, that 'none of

* Intervention of 29 April 1947.

the existing provisions of the powers of the executive [of the colonial government] has been done away with', and he was particularly exercised by the continuing reference to 'sedition', which had often been the justification used for the detention of freedom fighters by the colonial government. He wondered whether the conditions attached to the freedom of speech, for example, mightn't mean that he could be locked away simply for saying that the government of the day was doing something 'despicable'. He worried about the definition of 'grave emergency', and the possibility that 'anything that the party in power or the executive may not like would be considered a grave emergency' (which is more or less what happened in the 1975, with the declaration of Emergency rule, and the suspension of the fundamental rights, by the government of Indira Gandhi). Though not all the speakers agreed with Lahiri and other critics, Patel in response removed the specific provisos.

The Draft Constitution, however, made all the freedoms subject to a condition that nothing in the way they are defined should 'affect the operation of any existing law, or prevent the state from making any law' imposing restrictions on them: (i) in the case, specifically, of the freedom of speech and expression, because of 'offence against decency or morality', or 'undermining the authority or foundation of the state'; or, (ii) for all the other freedoms, 'in the interest of the general public'. These conditions were, therefore, comparable with those that appeared in the Interim Report. Again, there were members of the Assembly who expressed the view that the freedoms specified in the article were effectively taken away by the conditions attached to them. There were concerns, too, that the legislature was allowed too much power to pass new laws which would so undermine the rights that they would 'cease to be fundamental', in the words of one speaker. Dr Ambedkar, in response, pointed out that Article 8 of the Draft Constitution (Article 13 of the final version of 1950), which declares that any existing or future laws that are inconsistent with the provisions for the fundamental rights 'shall be void', guards against the possibility that these rights could be abrogated. But members of the Constituent Assembly continued to argue over who should have the last word, Parliament or the judges. In the end what became Article 19 was passed by the Assembly with one significant modification being the insertion throughout of the word 'reasonable' before the reference to 'restrictions'. This was held to provide a defence of the rights defined in the article—and to put the 'soul' back into it—because it implies that judicial judgement can be made of the appropriateness of restrictions. The second modification was the substitution of the reference to 'sedition' with a reference to undermining 'the sovereignty and integrity of India, the security of the State...'

It had been generally accepted in the Assembly that there had to be some limitations on the fundamental freedoms. The controversy was over how far they should be specified. The justification for the inclusion in the Constitution of so many limitations on the freedoms set out in Article 19 was put most clearly by Alladi Krishnaswamy Ayyar, the eminent Tamil lawyer who was one of the key figures in the writing of the Constitution. He summed up, on 8 November 1948, what he thought had emerged as the major criticisms of the Draft Constitution:

> The criticism regarding the fundamental rights was that they are hedged in by so many restrictions that no value can be attached to the rights guaranteed under the constitution. The great problem in providing for and guaranteeing fundamental rights in any constitution is where to draw the line between personal liberty and social control. True liberty can flourish only in a well ordered state and when the foundations of the state are not imperilled. The Supreme Court of the USA in the course of its long history has read a number of restrictions and limitations based upon the above principle into the rights expressed in wide and general terms. The Draft Constitution, instead of leaving it to the courts to read the necessary limitations and exceptions, seeks to express in a compendious form the limitations and exceptions recognised in any well ordered state. It cannot be denied that there is a danger

> in leaving the courts, by judicial legislation, so to speak, to read the necessary limitations, according to [the] idiosyncracies and prejudices...of individual judges.

The concern of the Drafting Committee was that if limits were not specified, and the courts were left with wide powers of interpretation then the rights might well end up by not amounting to very much at all. Better that they be specified rather than be left to the views of a few judges.

### *Article 21*

The language of the Interim Report, in what became Article 21, was that 'No person shall be deprived of his life or liberty without due process of law', and as Alladi Krishnaswamy Ayyar said in an early meeting of the Advisory Committee, the aim of 'due process' is to limit legislative power, because it allows the judiciary to question the law itself. The language that was finally agreed for Article 21—'procedure established by law'—is much more restrictive of the powers of the judges. What was at stake in the debate over the language of the article was whether it should invoke what is called 'procedural due process' or 'substantive due process'. The former refers to the power of the courts to review an action of the state and to examine whether it conforms to the statute that applies. Is the procedure required by the law being followed? For instance, if the law requires that the police hold a search warrant before entering a property, has this requirement been satisfied? 'Substantive due process', however, which is what the language used in the Interim Report implies, means that the courts have the power to consider the validity of the legislative enactment itself. Is the law itself fair and reasonable, or does it—in itself—violate the right to personal life and liberty? There is, clearly, a big difference between the two, and this is what was at issue in the controversy that took place in the Constituent Assembly over the Draft Constitution.

Initially, a majority of the Drafting Committee was in favour of retaining the language of 'due process', but ultimately it seems that the advice of B.N. Rau, the distinguished civil servant advising the Committee, who proposed the phrasing 'according to procedure established by law', prevailed. Rau had been influenced by his discussions with several senior lawyers in the United States whose views made him concerned about the possibility that too much power might be handed to a few judges. Members of the Drafting Committee were perhaps influenced by the insecurity in the country at the time, and by the shock of the assassination of Gandhi. A good many members of the Constituent Assembly, however, strongly advocated reversion to the language of 'due process'. The debate became heated. As one member argued, due process would mean that 'the judiciary will save us from the tyranny of the legislature and the executive'. In his response, on 13 December 1948, Dr Ambedkar, who as chairman of the Drafting Committee felt duty bound not to oppose the Committee's proposal—even though he was personally in favour of 'due process'—very unusually for him, sat on the fence. He said:

> For myself I cannot altogether omit the possibility of a Legislature packed by party men making laws which may abrogate or violate what we regard as certain fundamental principles affecting the life and liberty of an individual. At the same time, I do not see how five or six gentlemen sitting in the Federal or Supreme Court examining laws made by the Legislature and by dint of their own individual conscience or their bias or their prejudices be trusted to determine which law is good and which law is bad. It is rather a case where a man has to sail between Charybdis and Scylla and I therefore would not say anything.

He concluded, 'I would leave it to the House to decide in any way it likes.' The wording of the Draft was finally approved by the Assembly, though with unhappiness about it being widely felt.

Later, in September 1949, Ambedkar noted that '[n] o part of our Draft Constitution has been so violently criticized by the public outside' as what became Article 21. Criticism had its roots in the long history in colonial India of laws of preventive detention, and the passage, after 1947, in the provinces, of public order and safety acts which further allowed for detention, under conditions of varying stringency. While provision for preventive detention was generally thought to be necessary, there were widely shared fears about the possibility that legislatures would infringe on fundamental rights. Ambedkar referred, as well, to his own unhappiness, over the turn away from 'due process' in Article 15 of the Draft Constitution (finally Article 21). While Article 15 was included among the fundamental rights, 'we were giving a carte blanche to Parliament', he said, 'to make and provide for the arrest of any person under any circumstances as Parliament may think fit'. It was in response to these fears that Ambedkar introduced, on 15 September, a new article (15A), providing for regulation of detention so as to give some protection to those detained, even though parts of his proposal had been objected to by the Home Ministry. The new article (which eventually became Article 22 of the Constitution)—though in Austin's view, 'not as solicitous of individual liberty as Ambedkar claimed it to be'—was said by Ambedkar to provide for the substance of the law of 'due process'. It was intended, he said, as 'compensation for what was done in passing Article 15'. Further vigorous debate then took place but 15A was eventually passed.

Two months later, however, just ten days before the

Constituent Assembly concluded its work, an amendment was moved to 15A, and soon accepted, that embodied the views of the Home Ministry. Its effect was to reduce the authority of the courts and to reassert the powers of Parliament to detain people with much less protection provided by the judiciary than had been intended by Ambedkar in the new article. Article 22 excludes preventive detention cases from direct judicial scrutiny and creates, instead, an administrative review framework. Quite why Ambedkar did not challenge the amendment remains puzzling. Little was left of the protection that due process would have provided for personal freedom, and the historian of the Constitution, Granville Austin, summed up his account of these developments with the anxious words, 'The authority thus given to the Government of India is a potential danger to liberty.'

The Indian Constitution is one of very few constitutions around the world that explicitly permits preventive detention, and over the years, both Union and state governments have enacted many preventive detention laws, addressing matters ranging from national security to prevention of gambling and video piracy. Those detained have few rights and the courts have very little power to review detention orders. The official record shows that more than 12,000 people were in preventive detention in 2021.

**Liberties in Question**

In what follows here, I aim to document the main steps whereby successive governments of India have effectively undercut the 'golden triangle' of which CJI Chandrachud spoke, in spite of the efforts of some justices of the Supreme Court, such as Justice Chandrachud himself, to defend it. A few of the steps have had to do with securing social transformation. But it has been the demands of what have been held to be the needs of national security and integrity that have enabled governments to accumulate ever greater powers of repression. Liberty has been ever more threatened.

The freedoms specified in Article 19 were quickly put to test. In 1950 several court judgements to do with the freedom of expression (and of the press in particular) alarmed the central government, in the context of continuing fears over the security and integrity of the state. The insurgency in Telangana was still continuing in 1950, and many actual or supposed communists were in detention. Another court judgement, referring to the freedom of occupation, trade and business, conflicted with plans of the government of Uttar Pradesh for public ownership of bus services. Most important of all, because they challenged the government's determination to reform land tenure arrangements, were judgements regarding zamindari abolition, seen as being in conflict with the right to property. Thus it was that Parliament and the Supreme Court came into confrontation. The clashes between them had been anticipated in the Constituent Assembly debates, when some speakers had expressed their fears, as had Alladi Krishnaswamy Ayyar in the comment of his that I quoted earlier, that judicial review might place too much power into the hands of a few judges—with all their individual 'idiosyncracies and prejudices'. As I'll explain in chapter four, Nehru and others came firmly to believe that the judges stood in the way of the social reforms which they sought to bring about. Other members of the Constituent Assembly, however, had feared that a party with a majority in parliament might change the Constitution in line with the interests of particular groups in society (as we might now fear the influence on government of the interests of a few big business groups) and take away fundamental freedoms. The liberal constitutional principle of the separation of powers between the three branches of government, the executive, the legislature and the judiciary—to which the Constitution of India holds—is intended to guard against these possibilities, by having each branch provide a check on each of the others. But this system of checks and balances has come under strain quite often in India's history.

In 1951 Parliament amended the Constitution, using powers that it held (and holds still) under Article

368 (on 'Power of Parliament to amend the Constitution and procedure therefor'). The 1st Amendment empowered government to impose 'reasonable restrictions' on the freedom of expression; protected the right of the state to engage in a business even if it meant the exclusion of citizens from that business—their rights under Article 19 notwithstanding; and provided for the validation of laws for the abolition of the rights of zamindars. It also ensured that the right of equality should not bar government from enacting laws to benefit weaker sections of society—which had been threatened in a case brought by a young Brahmin woman (*State of Madras vs Srimathi Champakam Dorairajan*), on the grounds that despite her academic qualifications she would not be admitted to a medical school because of her caste and was therefore being discriminated against. But the significance of the amendment went far beyond its immediate objectives. As the historian Granville Austin put it, the amendment 'established the precedent of amending the Constitution to overcome judicial judgements impeding fulfilment of the government's perceived responsibilities'. An editorial of the *Times of India* (13 April 1951) argued that 'changes seem animated more by a desire to conserve the power of the executive than the rights of individuals'.

### *Contention Between Parliament and the Judiciary*

In the years that followed, the government passed other amendments that continued what had been started by the first, notably the 4th of 1955 and the 17th of 1964, which further consolidated the powers of government in regard to property, while the 16th of 1963 introduced further restrictions into Article 19 in the interests of national integrity—in the context, in particular, of the calls by the Tamil party, the Dravida Munnetra Kazhagam, for the establishment of a separate Dravidian state. The 16th Amendment was the foundation for the passage, in 1967, of the Unlawful Activities (Prevention) Act, first passed as a measure against secessionism. It has come to constitute perhaps the most serious threat of all to the liberty of Indian citizens in the 21st century. On this, more later.

The amendments of the 1950s and early 1960s brought, however, increased judicial scrutiny of the power of Parliament to amend the Constitution, and matters came to a head in 1967 over a case concerned with land rights in Punjab (the *Golaknath* case), when the Supreme Court ruled that the power of Parliament to amend the Constitution was subject to the restriction that it could not abridge any of the fundamental rights. Not long afterwards the court struck down two major policies of the government of Indira Gandhi—on the nationalization of banks, and the abolition of the 'purses' that had been paid to the rulers of the princely states. Both were held by the court to conflict with the right to property. The tensions between the government, with its socialist aims—as it claimed—and the court mounted. What should be the relationship between personal liberty and public good? How extensive were the powers of amendment that the Constitution allowed to Parliament? How, indeed, should an 'amendment' be defined? Debate became furious.

The 24th Amendment of the Constitution, passed in 1971, effectively re-asserted the right of Parliament to restrict the liberties of Article 19—in a move opposed by all the surviving members of the Constituent Assembly. It prompted *The Statesman* to argue in an editorial, 'The implications are breathtaking. Parliament now has the power to deny the seven freedoms [of the original Article 19].' This power was enhanced still more by the 25th Amendment of 1971, which further curtailed the right to property, and asserted the primacy of certain of the Directive Principles over the Fundamental Rights.

Then, in 1973, the Supreme Court fought back in its judgement on another case having to do with property rights, that of *Kesavananda Bharati*. The court's rulings were in favour of the government in so far as they overturned the anti-amendment conclusion of *Golaknath*, and they upheld the constitutionality of both the 24th and the 25th amendments. The ruling, however, that an amendment could not alter the 'basic structure' of the Constitution meant that the judgement as a whole was regarded as a defeat by the Indira Gandhi government. Seven of the 13 judges who sat on the case decided that Parliament's powers to amend were restricted to *modifying* the Constitution, and not to repealing or abrogating any parts of it in such a way as to change its 'fundamental identity' or basic features—or what came to be known as its 'basic structure'. This has never been explicitly defined by the judiciary, and has been held, at different times, to include the republican and democratic form of government, the unity and integrity of the nation, separation of powers, secularism, the federal character of the state—and the fundamental rights. Justice Khanna, in *Kesavananda*, for instance, did explicitly rule that the Fundamental Rights are among the 'basic features' of the Constitution.

The 'basic structure' doctrine has remained the cornerstone of interpretation of the Constitution, though it has not finally settled the problem of the respective powers of Parliament and the judiciary. The questions remain. How far can the government modify or restrict civil liberties? Can the judiciary strike down amendments passed by the legislature on the grounds that they violate the basic structure of the Constitution? Does the Constitution protect Indians from an 'abyss of unrestrained power'? These questions arose again in January 2023, when the

Vice President of India, Jagdeep Dhankhar, in the context of a continuing controversy over the procedure for the appointment of judges, argued in a speech that courts cannot dilute 'parliamentary sovereignty'. He did not agree, he said, with the idea that the judiciary can strike down amendments passed by the legislature on the grounds that they violate the 'basic structure' of the Constitution. The 'golden triangle' that defends Indian citizens from 'the abyss of unrestrained power', already greatly weakened, was under renewed threat.

The enduring significance of the *Kesavananda* judgement as the cornerstone of constitutional interpretation notwithstanding, it did not end the struggle between the government of Indira Gandhi and the court. In the context of her Emergency rule between 1975 and 1977, Mrs Gandhi's government passed into law the 42nd Amendment of 1976, so as (in the words of its text) 'to spell out expressly the high ideals of socialism, secularism and the integrity of the nation, to make the directive principles more comprehensive and give them precedence over the fundamental rights which have been allowed to be relied upon to frustrate socio-economic reforms'. To this end the Amendment sought above all 'to strengthen the presumption in favour of the constitutionality of legislation enacted by Parliament and State Legislatures'—which it did by making changes to the vital Article 368.

Unfortunately, in the judgement of most historians, the moves on Mrs Gandhi's part that culminated in the 42nd Amendment were driven much more by concern for the consolidation of her power than by the cause of social transformation. And none argue that the civil liberties provided for in the Constitution have been of much significance in accounting for the failures of social transformation. Responsibility, for instance, for the failure of land reform cannot be attributed to the judiciary. That responsibility clearly lay at the door of governments that relied heavily for support on local landed interests.

After the passing of the 42nd Amendment, however, Mrs Gandhi called fresh elections, and these brought the Morarji Desai-led Janata Party government into office in 1977. The new government promptly set about undoing the Emergency, and successfully repealed legislation that had curbed the freedoms of speech and of the press. It also provided for judicial independence—substantially overturned by Mrs Gandhi—and respected the principle of seniority in the appointment of the Chief Justice of India. In the 44th Amendment of the Constitution, in 1978, the government reversed provisions of the 42nd. The text of the Amendment ran, 'Recent experience has shown that the fundamental rights, including those of life and liberty, granted to citizens by the Constitution are capable of being taken away by a transient majority', and one of its primary objectives was to provide safeguards against a recurrence of this experience. It was also under the 44th Amendment that property ceased to be a fundamental right, to become only a legal right. The Law Minister, in proposing this clause argued that equating the right to property to 'more important things' (such, perhaps, as life and liberty) had resulted in the curbing of other fundamental rights.

### *India's Security Architecture, Powers of Repression*

The Janata government hedged, however, when it came to laws dealing with preventive detention—the subject, it will be remembered, of the new article that Ambedkar introduced late in the deliberations of the Constituent Assembly to make up for what he and many others saw as the limited protection offered to liberty by Article 21. As I noted earlier, Ambedkar's stated intentions were effectively undermined by a last-minute amendment to the article that was urged by the Home Ministry. Then, under the first Preventive Detention Act, passed in February 1950, only 30 days after the promulgation of the Constitution, the courts were forbidden from questioning the necessity for any detention order. The Act was tested in the case of the communist leader, A.K. Gopalan, who, having been in detention since December 1947, was further detained by the Government of Madras under the Preventive Detention Act. Gopalan made a number of claims against the Madras government, including the claim that the provisions of the Act violated Article 22 of the Constitution. The judgement of a bench of the Supreme Court, however, upheld the legislation and the powers of the government. The Preventive Detention Act was then extended a number of times before it finally expired in 1969—to be replaced by a series of further acts of Parliament providing for preventive detention. A standard justification, in the words of a Congress Parliamentary Party pamphlet, was that public order comes first, 'then all endeavours to promote social welfare are possible and practicable'. Legislation under Article 22 became progressively more stringent, and was reinforced during the national emergencies of 1962, when India fought with China, and of 1971, in the conflict with Pakistan.

The Indira Gandhi government passed the Maintenance of Internal Security Act (MISA) in 1971. Based on the Preventive Detention Act, MISA allowed for the indefinite preventive detention of individuals, search and seizure of property without warrants, and for wire-tapping, with the stated objective of the quelling of disorder and meeting external threats to national security. The Act was used, infamously, during the Emergency to justify the arrests of political opponents, and many thousands of people were detained for long periods. The Janata Party had pledged its repeal, and did so in 1978, when the government also passed the 44th Amendment that was supposed to provide for safeguards against a recurrence of the Emergency. Of particular significance were the safeguards added to Article 22 to tackle what the law minister called the 'evil' of preventive detention. The Janata government, however, even after drawing up the 44th Amendment, argued for the value of the instrument of preventive detention in countering economic offences (such as black marketing), as well as in protecting national security. The relevant section 3 of the 44th Amendment, making for independent judicial review of preventive detention orders, has still not been enforced, more than forty years after its passage in 1978. Successive governments have failed to bring the amendment of Article 22 into force, as an open letter, submitted in 2021 by one hundred former civil servants to the law minister, pointed out. They asked that it be 'notified' (the term means the enforcement of a constitutional amendment), in the context of what the signatories of the letter described as 'brazen abuse of preventive detention laws in gross violation of human rights'.

Mrs Gandhi returned to power in 1980, and in the same year her government passed the National Security Act which empowered the central and state governments to detain a person so as to prevent him or her from acting in a manner held to be prejudicial to the security of the country. The Act was widely criticized as an instrument of repression, and Granville Austin described the period that ensued after the passage of the act as one in which 'liberties were lost'. Abuses of the powers of preventive detention are common.

There has been, it is said, a sustained tendency for the consolidation of India's security architecture, in what has been represented by successive governments as a continuing state of threat to the nation's integrity and security. Extraordinary laws have been passed, in order to address 'crimes of terror', giving governments even stronger powers to detain people without having to go through steps that provide citizens with some protection against the arbitrary exercise of state power. The Terrorist and Disruptive Activities (Prevention) Act (TADA) was passed in 1985 to address the Khalistani Movement in Punjab, but it came to be applied to the whole of India, till it lapsed in 1995. Strongly criticized by human rights organizations, for including provisions that violate human rights, in the end less than two per cent of those arrested under TADA were convicted. It was followed by the Prevention of Terrorism Act (POTA), which included similar provisions to TADA, after the attack on the Indian parliament in December 2001. POTA was replaced in turn by the UAPA Amendment Act 2004, which was then subject to further amendments, most recently in 2019, always in the direction of increasing the arbitrary powers of the government. This string of laws is based on the presumption that those accused are guilty unless it can be proven to the contrary, in an inversion of the normal process of law. These repressive laws have been drawn on by all political regimes and governments, at the centre and in the states.

In addition to this more recent repressive legislation, the Armed Forces (Special Powers) Act (AFSPA) enacted in April 1958 to suppress the Naga insurgency, subsequently extended for a long period to the whole of the Northeast, later to Punjab and, from 1990, to Jammu and Kashmir, has for long been used to deny the people of these parts of the country their basic civil liberties. They have lived in a more or less permanent 'state of exception', it may be said, when they are denied what are usually accepted as being the rights of Indian citizens in the rest of the country. The Act empowers governments to declare that a state or a union territory or particular areas have become 'disturbed' and 'dangerous', so that it is necessary to use the armed forces 'in aid of civil power'. AFSPA has shifted powers of normal policing to the army in Kashmir, for long periods in the Northeast, and in those areas of central and eastern India most affected by Maoist insurgency, even while making officers from the armed forces immune from 'prosecution, suit or other legal proceeding'. There have been many occasions when it has been claimed, often with compelling evidence, that these powers have been abused.

## A Brief Conclusion

In sum, there is no doubt that the liberty—in the sense of 'freedom from arbitrary, despotic or autocratic control'—promised by the 'golden triangle' of Articles 14, 19 and 21 of the Constitution has been severely compromised, in significant part by the kind of Trojan Horse among the fundamental rights that is Article 22. Austin's fear that '[t]he authority [it gave] to the Government of India is a potential danger to liberty', has been amply justified by events. There has been a strong tendency, almost from the time that the Constitution first came into force, for governments to assume arbitrary powers, and to resist judicial review of legislation and of their use of such instruments as preventive detention orders. Some of this has been driven—certainly in the early days of the new republic when the government was trying to bring about agrarian reforms—by the objective of realizing the social transformation promised by the Constitution. But from the beginning, and perhaps understandably, given the challenges to national unity and security that India faced in the later 1940s and 1950s, it has been what have been represented, at least, as threats to unity and security, that have justified the restriction of liberties and violations of human rights. It is argued by lawyers that the preventive detention laws of the post-colonial state in India are often harsher than those of the colonial state. Liberties have been lost. Have the claims of national integrity and security, and the demands of economic and social reform, finally torn apart the 'seamless web' of the Constitution? These are questions for chapter five.

# Intermezzo*

## Liberty in Everyday Life

The Constitution of India offers a programme—outlined in the Resolution on Aims and Objects that began the deliberations of the Constituent Assembly—for the transformation of a deeply hierarchical society. India was to be rebuilt through the establishment of a civic community in which individuals are the bearers of equal civil, political and social rights. Yet, as Dr Ambedkar argued while introducing the Draft Constitution in November 1948, 'Constitutional morality is not a natural sentiment. It has to be cultivated. We must realize that our people are yet to learn it. Democracy in India is only a top-dressing on an Indian soil, which is essentially undemocratic.' How far have the civil and political liberties promised by the Constitution, and that are an essential foundation

* An intermezzo means 'a performance inserted between the acts of a play', but here it is a short essay between the chapters of the book.

of a democracy, transformed Indian society? What can be learnt, in answer to this question, from the work of sociologists and other scholars who have studied Indian society in depth?

From the 1940s through to the 1970s a lot of social scientists studied villages in different parts of the country, influenced by the idea—shared by Gandhi—that the villages, where the great majority of Indians then lived (and still do) are the foundation of Indian society as a whole. Or they saw the village as a microcosm of the society. Their work showed up, as we might expect, many differences across the country, and yet they also found much the same fundamental structure. The intersection of hereditary status differences bound up with caste and class differences, principally those between substantial landowners, their tenants, more or less independent peasant household farmers, and those relying on wage labour alone, created extensive dependency among people. As the leading Indian sociologist of his time, M.N. Srinivas, wrote in an article about the Karnataka village where he had lived and studied, 'No account of a village social system can be complete without reference to certain institutionalized vertical relationships between individuals and, through them, between families. These relationships include the relations of master and servant, landowner and tenant, and creditor and debtor; they may be viewed collectively as the relationships of patrons and clients.' The leading landowners, almost invariably from castes ranked relatively high up the scale, exercised dominance in the villages, constraining the freedoms of the majority because of their control over resources and their privileged access to the state. They might be benevolent patrons, but their clients lived always with the possibility of their livelihoods being threatened. They lived in the shadow of coercion. This was true of none more so than the Dalits, and some tribal people, who suffered from discrimination in many spheres of social life and who were mostly dependent upon labouring for others under conditions that were often not very different from the outright servitude that the forefathers of many of them had known. Many remained tied to particular landowners through debt which might be carried over generations. But life was a struggle for survival for most other people, too. This was a kind of 'survival society'. These were not conditions in which there was much solidarity or cooperation between people. There was solidarity, perhaps, within particular groups, usually defined by caste, but the idea of fraternity was a distant ideal in a society that had such deep divisions and differences. And, of course, it was a patriarchal society in which women were expected to be subservient to men.

These were conditions that the Constitution was intended to change, through the provisions in the

Fundamental Rights, among them the elimination of discrimination (including discrimination on grounds of sex), of untouchability, and of all forms of forced labour; through the right of democratic participation in local councils and in state and national elections; and through the Directive Principles, with their instructions to governments intended to ensure that all Indians are able to lead lives with dignity and self-respect. How has it worked?

Even as the sociologists to whose work I have referred were researching in villages across the country, changes were taking place. One of the early studies, of a village in eastern Uttar Pradesh in the late 1940s, seemed to reach some very positive conclusions: 'the mass education of untouchable children [they made up 50 per cent of all school children in the village in 1949]; the introduction of co-education; the tolerance of widow remarriage; the wresting of political power from the landowners and high caste groups by the artisans and lower castes—these are momentous changes that penetrate to the core of village life, and indeed, of Indian life'. And, the authors said, 'The realization that every one of them had the same right to vote as the wealthiest man in the village, has filled them with great hope about a vaguely conceived future.' Other studies, too, showed that the kind of dominance exercised historically by the leading landowners and the upper castes was breaking down. They no longer, for example, had the authority they once had, to adjudicate disputes within and among the lower-caste groups, nor always the power to enforce caste privilege. The old moral order of village society unquestionably was broken down, according to village studies, by the individualistic ideology of representative democracy. There was a lot of hope in the early years of the new republic, in the possibilities of democracy, and of much greater freedom, both positive (through education, for instance) and negative (being less subject to the cudgel of the landlord, for example).

Local tyrannies were reduced, no question, in the new republic, but this didn't mean the emergence of the new social and political order, attuned to the interests of the least privileged Indians, that the Founders promised in the Constitution. There has been social progress, of course, but discrimination remains a big problem, on grounds of caste, of gender and religion; large numbers of labourers, even including children sometimes, still are bound to employers by debt and may be subject to terrible conditions of employment, including physical beating; if there was once great hope in the possibilities of democratic politics, it has perhaps been lost, for politics is seen, with reason, as a dirty business; the police are widely feared—sensibly so—rather than being seen as upholders of law and order; and while living conditions have improved very significantly, thanks in large measure to interventions by the state that have provided for much greater social protection, very large numbers still live their lives in and out of poverty. The long-running failures of successive governments to invest in education and in basic health care, and their failures to make these public services work, continue to blight the prospects of very many Indians.

The salience of caste differences in Indian society and politics remains significant, reflected, for instance, in the controversy over whether or not there should be a new caste census. The persistence of discrimination against Dalits and tribal people is reflected in notorious incidents, even in a state such as Tamil Nadu, often considered to be among the more progressive in the country. On an everyday level, there are indications, for instance, from Tamil Nadu of Dalits being refused tea in village tea shops, where once they were allowed in, and there are a good many cases of their exclusion from village temples, sometimes leading to violence. Their continuing exclusion from some of the 'better' jobs is also significant, and they are often restricted to the least well-paid as well as the most demeaning forms of employment. They are likely to be disproportionately included among the so-called 'footloose' labour, compelled to find work through migration on a permanent or a seasonal basis, and still very often under conditions of debt-bondage. It may not be 'forced labour' in quite the same forms as those of the past, but these are forms of employment that may limit basic freedoms. Gender discrimination is marked in many ways, not least in the low level of female participation in the labour force, as well as in the adverse sex ratio. The relatively low numbers of women in the population of large parts of the country is a clear marker of discrimination against them, even before birth. The increasing significance of religious discrimination is suggested in the findings of social anthropologists who have recently done restudies in three of the villages (one each in Gujarat, Odisha and Madhya Pradesh) where some of the more important research of the mid-twentieth century was carried on. The anthropologists refer to the idea of 'incivility', meaning forms of collective hostility and discrimination, and they say that incivility now appears in the public realm of the villages most significantly between Hindus and Muslims or between Hindus and Christians. So, they find, 'while the incivility of caste remains strong, the language and logic of discrimination based on religious allegiances have moved to the fore'. In sum, the civic community envisaged in the Constitution appears to be as remote as ever.

And what of the hopes inspired by the beginnings of democratic politics, such as those that were observed by those who studied the village in eastern UP in the late 1940s? Only a little later, studies of village politics showed the existence of 'vote blocs' that could be mobilized by locally influential, powerful individuals through ties of obligation and dependence. Such men could deliver blocs of votes to candidates in elections in return for benefits such as access to lucrative public works contracts. Or they might secure office for themselves with the same objectives. The cynicism about politics as a 'dirty business' that is widely noted often appears to be justified, and is also a marker of the limited development of a sense of civic responsibility.

Subsequent research has shown that the capacities of village elites to deliver or to draw on blocs of votes from those dependent upon them in some way have declined considerably, and that poorer people—for whom the simple act of voting is important in itself as a statement of their citizenship—vote as they wish and increasingly in response to the direct appeals of politicians. There is still a lot of evidence, however, both from cities and from rural India, of the significance of intermediaries who function as 'brokers' between politicians and the electorate, and who are able to influence voting at least to some extent. And there is evidence, too, that criminal bosses can command electoral majorities in what has been called 'mafia raj'. In these ways, too, the fears that Dr Ambedkar expressed seem to have been borne out. The 'constitutional morality' of which he spoke remains a tender plant. Some observers think, indeed, that the alignment between the objectives of the Constitution and the reality of Indian society has increasingly gone awry.

# Chapter IV

# A Glass Half Full?

## Positive Freedoms

### What Happened to Social and Economic Rights in the Constitution?

K.T. Shah—described by Granville Austin as 'perhaps the most doctrinaire socialist in the Constituent Assembly'—in a note for colleagues on the Sub-Committee on Fundamental Rights, argued that economic and social rights providing, broadly, for freedom from want, were indispensable, because without them, civil and political rights would be meaningless: 'The right to free elections without a full belly would be a mockery.' Shah's colleague on the Sub-Committee, one of the most influential members of the Constituent Assembly, K.M. Munshi, who was strongly inclined to the Right (and later one of the founders of the conservative Swatantra Party), was also supportive of judicially enforceable rights. He proposed the inclusion of rights of workers (including rights to work and social security) and the right to education. These views were in line with what had been proposed in both the Nehru Report of 1928 and the Karachi Resolution of the Congress of 1931, discussed in chapter two. Both had argued, in effect, that the right to well-being is an essential precondition for the right to life and liberty. Shah's and Munshi's views were expressed, too, at a moment of India's history in the later 1940s, when there had been massive agitations and protests articulating demands for distributive justice. There were rural rebellions, especially the Tebhaga Movement in eastern India, and the peasant uprising in Telangana. There were protests by students, and most significantly massive strikes, mostly led by the Communist Party of India, of miners, railwaymen, postal workers, bank employees and even of the police. In the last days of their rule the British thought, indeed, that it was perfectly possible that there would be a well-organized revolution in 1946. In this context it does seem surprising that, in the end, social and economic rights were 'relegated', as several writers have put it, to the Directive Principles of State Policy.

The case against creating judicially enforceable rights to livelihood, health and education, such as would supply positive freedoms, was put in the note by the

Constitutional Adviser, B.N. Rau, quoted in chapter two. He argued that there are rights that can be enforced by law essentially because they require the state to refrain from certain actions. But how can the state ensure—in the example that Rau gave—that there is full employment so that all can secure their livelihoods? Can a right to work be enforced by the courts? Potential rights, or freedoms, that require positive action by the state, may simply be impractical. Eventually it was agreed by the Sub-Committee that a distinction should be made between those rights that clearly are judicially enforceable, civil and political rights, and those—social rights—which, it was held, are not enforceable in the courts. Thus, in his letter to the Assembly President of 23 April 1947, Patel, as the Chair of the Advisory Committee submitting the Interim Report on Fundamental Rights, drew attention to its recommendation 'that the list of fundamental rights should be prepared in two parts, the first part consisting of rights enforceable by appropriate legal process and the second consisting of directive principles of state policy which, though not enforceable in courts, are nonetheless to be regarded as fundamental in the governance of the country'.

The distinction that was being made was not directly challenged in the debate on the Interim Report, though the communist, Somnath Lahiri, argued that 'it is rather difficult to make a fine distinction between what are justiciable rights and what are not', and P.R. Thakur insisted that economic rights must be made justiciable. It was when Ambedkar introduced the Draft Constitution, more than a year later, and the Directive Principles were laid out before the Assembly for the first time, that the distinction was questioned in an awkward debate.

Ambedkar's own role in this is a puzzle. In his Memorandum and Draft Articles on the Rights of States and Minorities (submitted to the Advisory Committee on Fundamental Rights, Minorities, and Tribal and Excluded Areas on 24 March 1947) he had made a passionate case for a socialist economic structure, and he had challenged lawyers to think differently about economic and social rights. 'Time has come', he wrote, 'to take a bold step and define both the economic structure as well as the political structure of society by the law of the constitution.' Yet when he introduced the Draft Constitution, in November 1948, he presented the reasoned argument for placing these rights in the non-justiciable Directive Principles—without offering any explanation for the apparent change in his views. Perhaps Ambedkar the astute politician, recognizing the conservatism of the prominent lawyers in the Constituent Assembly, such as Alladi Krishnaswamy Ayyar, and indeed the conservative character of a majority of the members, knew that this was a battle he could not win, and that 'half a loaf' was better than none. At least, with the statement in the Constitution of the Directive Principles, the demands of the social transformation of India could not be forgotten—and the legislation of social rights in this century, which I'll discuss later in this chapter, seems to justify this interpretation of Ambedkar's actions. It is also possible that Ambedkar the lawyer struggled with the tension between his commitment to parliamentary democracy on the one hand and to socialism on the other. He spoke subsequently of the constitution as providing a framework for democracy and argued that it must be for democratically elected governments to determine the design of public policy. In response to an amendment proposed by K.T. Shah that would have had the commitment to socialism included in the Preamble to the Constitution, Ambedkar said, 'What should be the policy of the State, how the Society should be organized on its social and economic side, are matters which should be decided by the people themselves according to time and circumstances. It cannot be laid down in the Constitution itself because that is destroying democracy altogether' (15 November 1948). This is a statement that seems in conflict with what he'd said in his earlier Memorandum, but we have no direct evidence on why Ambedkar apparently changed his views. The Directive Principles seem to have constituted for him a working compromise. In defining the social aims that all governments should strive to satisfy, the Constitution would ensure that social rights could not be ignored.

In the debate in the Constituent Assembly that followed Ambedkar's introduction of the Draft Constitution there were those who argued that unless the 'directives' were made justiciable they would be merely 'platitudes or pious wishes'. K.T. Shah argued that the principles should be 'mandatory, compulsory obligations of the state, which every citizen will have the right to demand should be fulfilled'. There were those who thought that the Directive Principles did not go nearly far enough towards the establishment of socialism and others who regretted language such as that the State should 'strive to' achieve the various objectives of policy. The Gandhian activist, Mahavir Tyagi, for instance, argued, 'When we try to put something real in the Constitution, why should these lawyers come between our wishes and the Constitution? They should make it absolutely plain that the purpose of the Constitution is to secure justice, social, political and economic.'

On the other hand, there were members such as Ananthasayanam Ayyangar whose view was that 'We must be practical'. If, for example, the stated aim of there being free and compulsory primary education for all within ten years were not to be achieved, what could the courts do about it? It couldn't be in the power of the courts to dismiss a democratically elected government. No, he argued, the real sanction lies in the democratic process. The people would sanction a government that failed to realize such an objective by voting them out of office: 'That is the real sanction, and not the sanction of any court of law.' Mahboob Ali Baig argued that 'directive principles' should have no place in the Constitution. He found them contrary to the principles of parliamentary democracy. What if a party that pursues principles contrary to those set out is elected into office? 'Is it the purpose of these principles to bind and tie down the political parties in the country to a certain programme...? Surely not, that will not be democracy.' This was almost exactly what Ambedkar had argued against K.T. Shah just four days earlier. On this occasion Ambedkar offered no magisterial summing up and judgement to conclude the debate.

Baig's intervention sharply exposed the fuzziness in the status of the Directive Principles. Not judicially enforceable rights but still 'instructions' to government? How should this work in a democracy? Still, given the broad commitment of the Constituent Assembly to social and economic rights, but with the recognition, too, of the problems of practicality and enforceability, the Directive Principles were allowed. No doubt some members were relieved by this outcome. We should remember that the Congress party that supplied by far the most members was not a revolutionary organization, but—not least with its dependence by this time on local landed interests—one inclined to conservatism. This was shown in the latter days of the freedom struggle when, on a number of occasions, the Congress leadership stopped agitations when they threatened, for example, to spill over from protests against the land revenue imposed by the colonial state into campaigns against the payment of rent. Later, in the early years of the republic, the interests of the rich peasants on whom the Congress relied for electoral support ensured that measures to bring about redistributive land reform and cooperative farming—advocated by a fraction of the party's leadership—were frustrated.

In this chapter, I will go on to discuss what has happened to the Directive Principles and the positive freedoms that they promised, in the working of the Constitution and in the context of India's particular pattern of economic and social development. After decades in which very little was achieved, more recent developments with what has been called a 'new rights agenda' have perhaps filled the glass of positive freedom half full.

## Directive Principles Versus Fundamental Rights

A critical question that came up in some of the most heated debates in the Constituent Assembly was that of the respective powers of the executive, Parliament and the judiciary, as we saw in chapter three. This was what the argument over 'due process' in regard to Article 21 was all about. As it turned out, a good deal of the confrontation between the executive and the judiciary in the early years of independent India had to do with the relationship of the fundamental rights and the directive principles. The latter were expressions of the objective of social transformation promised in the Preamble, and conflict arose particularly when policies that the government wanted to adopt to carry forward this objective were found by the courts to be infringing upon the fundamental rights—mostly the right to property.

It was widely recognized by India's political leaders, well before the first meetings of the Constituent Assembly, that in the primarily agrarian country that India still was, land tenure arrangements—including both the distribution of land ownership and the incidence of crippling rack-renting of land—stood in the way of the social transformation that they wanted to bring about. As Nehru said, speaking on 10 September 1949 to the article in the Draft Constitution concerned with compulsory acquisition of property, '[N]othing is more important and vital than a gradual reform of the big estates'—and even as he was speaking, legislation about the big estates (of the tax-farming zamindars) was under discussion in Bihar, the United Provinces and Madras. But then, how were the major changes that had to be brought about to be reconciled with the right to property? There was a lengthy debate in the Constituent Assembly, justifying Nehru's observation, 'I doubt if there are many other articles which have given rise to so much discussion and debate'. There was much argument over the question of compensation for property that was taken over. What was economically feasible and morally just? Then there was the question of which of the institutions of government should be the final arbiter, Parliament or the Supreme Court.

The Constitution was soon put to test. Among other developments in 1950 there were court judgements challenging the government's determination to reform land tenure arrangements through zamindari abolition as being in conflict with the right to property. An unfavourable ruling on this of the High Court of Bihar led Nehru to argue that 'if the Constitution itself comes in our way, then surely it is time to change the Constitution'.* He had said even in the course of the deliberations of the Constituent Assembly, on 10 September 1949, that 'no individual could override the rights of the community', and as events unfolded very soon after the promulgation of the Constitution, the objectives of social transformation that he had set out in the first debate of the Constituent

* Letter to Chief Ministers, 1 February 1951.

Assembly came into conflict with the individual liberties of Article 19. Nehru was to say later that if the courts found a contradiction between the Fundamental Rights and the Directive Principles, then 'it is up to Parliament to remove the contradiction and make the Fundamental Rights subserve the Directive Principles of State Policy'.*

Parliament and the Supreme Court increasingly came into confrontation. The battle between the judiciary and the executive became 'embalmed' (in the felicitous phrasing of Niraja Gopal Jayal) as one between individual rights and the requirements of social justice. The government regularly used its powers of constitutional amendment to overturn adverse decisions of the court. The 25th Amendment of 1971, brought by the Indira Gandhi government, as well as taking away from the Supreme Court the power to intervene in setting compensation in cases of the taking over of property, introduced a new article, 31C, into the Constitution. This exempted from judicial review any law intended to secure—or even a law claiming to be intended to secure—certain of the principles set out under Article 39, among the Directive Principles, even if the law violated fundamental rights. The particular principles concerned were (i) that the ownership and control of material resources should serve the common good, and (ii) that the

* Lok Sabha Debates, 14 March 1955.

functioning of the economy shouldn't be such as to result in concentration of wealth and of means of production, to the 'common detriment'. These are important socialist principles, but the background to the passage of the amendment was not so much commitment to these principles, as the determination to overturn decisions of the Supreme Court against the government, on the matter of bank nationalization. Subsequently, in the expansive 42nd Amendment of 1976, the wording of Article 31C was changed in such a way as to assert the primacy of all the directive principles over the fundamental rights.

The relevant clause (clause 4) of the 42nd Amendment was then struck down, however, in the judgement of the Supreme Court in the *Minerva Mills* case in 1980. The court ruled the clause to be unconstitutional. The judgement, more widely, reaffirmed the court's view that the Constitution confers only limited powers of amendment to Parliament, so applying and developing further the 'basic structure' doctrine about which I wrote in chapter three. It was in the context of this judgement that Chief Justice Chandrachud wrote of the 'golden triangle' constituted by Articles 14, 19 and 21, standing between liberty and the 'abyss of unrestrained power', which I have referred to earlier. He argued that Article 31C had had the effect of removing two sides of the triangle (Articles 19 and 21)—so threatening the liberty of Indian citizens.

In more recent years, as I will discuss later in this chapter, the directive principles and the fundamental rights have rather become complementary to one another, as the courts have read various social and economic rights into Article 21. First, a note on how far the directive principles have been effective.

**Have the Directive Principles Influenced State Policy?**

The answer to this question must be 'not very much'. The Directive Principles together 'instruct' Indian governments to provide for freedom from want for all Indians, and to give them access to education and to health care, so that they can lead lives with dignity. A great deal of progress has been made, as analyses of the declining incidence of poverty demonstrate, but it is also well known that very many Indians lead lives in which they move in and out of poverty, as I point out in the 'Intermezzo' that precedes this chapter. In terms of most indicators of well-being, India now lags behind its neighbour, Bangladesh, once thought of as the archetypal 'basket-case' among the countries of the world. The overwhelming judgement of economists and other specialists, whether from right or left, is that India has done very much less well than it might have done, because of policy choices that have been made.

The whole pattern of economic development has

not been one in which the fruits of growth are fairly distributed (as Articles 38 and 39 say they should have been), or distributed in such a way as to encourage further development. While it may be entirely understandable, given the state of the economy at the time of Independence, and the prevailing orthodoxy of the nascent discipline of development economics, that governments in the 1950s should have given priority to economic growth through rapid, capital-intensive industrialization, it is clear—with the advantage of hindsight—that policy makers did not focus nearly enough on employment. They missed out on the possibilities for the employment-intensive pattern of industrialization that was taken up in East Asian economies with such success. As it has turned out, the pattern of India's economic development has been distinctly dualistic, and a very large share of the labour force, and a significant share of all production, is in the so-called 'informal sector', where workers have few rights and limited incomes. Economic growth has simply failed to create genuine economic opportunity for all.

Policy makers also didn't focus nearly enough on the agricultural economy in which the great majority of Indians then worked (and still do, even if agriculture, on average, directly makes up a smaller share of rural incomes than work in other activities). Agrarian reform such as might have led to the growth of productivity with and through fairer distribution of land and other resources, didn't happen. Policy makers also neglected education. The failure to realize the intention stated in Article 45, of achieving universal primary education within ten years (that was, by 1960), is perhaps the most egregious failure of all of successive governments. It is probably true that far too many officials at different levels, over the years, mainly from upper castes, have held the view that the masses don't really need much education. Another terrible failure has been in regard to health care. In this sphere, too, India sadly still lags comparator countries. In sum, it really is hard to justify the idea that the ideals of the directive principles have had very much influence at all on state policy, at any moment in the history of independent India.

The emphasis in India's economic policy has always been on economic growth, and perhaps increasingly so, as the size and rate of growth of the economy have assumed such importance for the country's geopolitical ambitions. Yet, at the same time, the scale of poverty has always been an embarrassment to those same ambitions, and successive governments have introduced many different programmes to tackle the problem, starting with the Community Development Programme of Nehru's time, and continuing with such interventions as the poverty-focused Integrated Rural Development Programme, or the requirement that banks should give priority in lending to sectors where the poor would, it was believed, benefit most. With all of these programmes, research studies showed that benefits had a frustrating way of filtering upwards, into the hands of those with some local power. The poverty programmes were in the way of being compensatory, philanthropic measures, and they did little to address the livelihood problems of the very large numbers of Indians who were, effectively, excluded from the dynamic, productive sectors of the economy. Economic growth was supposed to make everybody better off, but the 'benefits of growth' have filtered down only very slowly, at best. If people are to move out of the shadow of poverty then they must have access to education of reasonable quality, and to affordable health care. Education certainly doesn't guarantee social mobility, but without it people's prospects are generally severely limited. The importance of access to health care is shown in careful research that demonstrates the significance of episodes of ill-health in pushing people into poverty. Yet, throughout the history of independent India, right up to the present day, governments have failed to invest adequately in education and health care, which might have done so much to provide for positive freedoms.

Then, in the later 20th century and especially in the first decade and a half of the present one, the judges of the Supreme Court, responding mainly to pressures from groups within civil society, gradually whittled away the distinction between the Fundamental Rights and the Directive Principles. Judgements of the Supreme Court, extending back over many years—some its most progressive rulings were made in the early to mid-1980s—have in effect rendered some non-enforceable Directive Principles justiciable in a court, and upgraded the status of elementary education, at least, to that of fundamental right. It has been interpretations of Article 21, on 'right to protection of life and liberty', that have been especially significant. Those who drafted this article may have had in mind protection against arbitrary arrest and detention, but the judges have interpreted it to mean 'the right to live with human dignity and all that goes along with it, namely, the bare necessities of life, such as adequate nutrition'—in the words, for example, of a Supreme Court judgement of 1981 (*Francis Coralie Mullin vs The Administrator, Union Territory of Delhi*). The objectives set out in Part IV of the Constitution, promising positive freedoms, became more of a focus in public policy than they had been before.

**The 'New Rights Agenda'**

The 'new rights agenda', as it has been called, came about largely as a result of pressures from within civil society, and generally in interaction with judicial activism. The best-known of these policy innovations is the Mahatma Gandhi National Rural Employment Guarantee Scheme—

legislated for in 2005 (in the National Rural Employment Guarantee Act [NREGA]). The world's largest rights-based safety net programme, MGNREGS gives all rural households the *right* to up to 100 days of guaranteed wage employment per year, at an agreed minimum wage. In 2005, as well, the Right to Information Act (RTI) was passed, making it mandatory for government agencies to release information about their activities to individual citizens upon request. The Right to Information is foundational to the whole rights agenda because, as has been argued on its website by the Mazdur Kisan Shakti Sangathan (MKSS), which initiated the struggle for this right, 'transparency and accountability of systems of governance are basic to access any right'.

A year after the passage of NREGA and the RTI, the Scheduled Tribes and Other Traditional Forest Dwellers (Recognition of Forest Rights) Act, 2006 gave tribal communities and other forest dwellers rights in the forests that had been denied to them before. Then the Right of Children to Free and Compulsory Education Act, 2009 made the enrolment, attendance and completion of schooling of every child up to the age of 14 the obligation of the state. The National Food Security Act—which is designed to guarantee that people will not go hungry, by providing foodgrains at low and regulated prices to about two-thirds of the population—was passed in 2013.

The drivers of the new rights agenda were not politicians and political parties—though the United Progressive Alliance (UPA) government of 2004–14 created an important space for policy innovation, beneath the umbrella of the National Advisory Council (NAC). This was set up by the Congress president, Sonia Gandhi, to oversee the implementation of the Common Minimum Programme (CMP) that the Congress, heading the Alliance, agreed with its coalition partners and with the left parties (supporting the government on the outside), and which promised 'growth with a human face'. The new welfare architecture that was created wasn't the outcome of extensive popular mobilization. It was rather the result of lobbying by civil society activists, and of judicial intervention—the two having tended to work together.

The origins of MGNREGS are shared with those of the more recent, much more fiercely contested right to food, finally established with the Food Security Act of 2013. A Supreme Court judgement of November 2001, in a case brought by the Peoples Union for Civil Liberties (PUCL) against the Government of India, through the instrument of public interest litigation—in a context in which there was famine in parts of Rajasthan, at a time when it was very well known that the Food Corporation of India held massive stocks of foodgrains—explicitly established a constitutional right to food. The court held that government food schemes—the Targeted Public Distribution System, the Midday Meals Scheme for schools and the Integrated Child Development Services programme—constituted legal entitlements; it set out minimum allocation levels of foodgrains and supplemental nutrients for the poor; and it outlined how these government schemes were to be implemented. Essentially, the court's judgement rested on the view that the right to life under Article 21 includes the right to food.

Subsequently the relationships between the judiciary, the Right to Food Campaign—a loose coalition of civil society groups, the establishment of which was stimulated by the action of the PUCL in bringing its case—and the commissioners whom the Court required to be appointed to oversee the implementation of its orders, worked quite effectively, and in such a way as to act at least as a check upon actions of the government intended to deregulate and liberalize the economy, where these moves conflicted with food security. The struggle that went on over the Food Security Act for several years showed up, however, how strong the opposition was from many in government to the objectives of the Right to Food campaigners, because of what was believed to be the cost of food security, and because of the evidence of high levels of leakage from the Public Distribution System—when foodstuffs are sold off privately to the profit of ration-shop owners and others.

The same civil society activists who demanded the right to food were influential in the decision of Congress leaders to include the idea of the employment guarantee in the party's manifesto for the 2004 election, and subsequently in the Common Minimum Programme. Key activists with the Right to Food campaign, who were also members of the National Advisory Council, presented a draft bill at its first meeting. There was subsequently considerable conflict between different government departments over the bill, with both the Ministry of Finance and the Planning Commission questioning the financial feasibility of a national employment guarantee. The Act that was finally passed, however, after a struggle on the part of the activists, included most of the provisions in the original proposals. The National Food Security Act, on the other hand, fell short of what the campaigners had sought.

The story of the passage of the Right to Education Act (RtE) includes a similar set of factors. This Act, too, was forged outside the realm of electoral politics. Successive governments of India for long failed to allocate sufficient resources or attention to honour the mandate upon the state of Article 45 of the Constitution, that government should 'endeavour' to provide free and compulsory education to all children up to the age of 14 within a period of ten years. A succession of committees and reports, over many years, have advocated that resources equivalent to at least 6 per cent of GDP should be spent on education. But education expenditure, as a share of GDP, has rarely reached four per cent, way below the international average, and below the levels of expenditure in countries that compare most closely with India. The National Education Policy of 2020, and then the New National Education Policy of 2023 have both stated the aim that the outlay for education should increase to 6 per cent of GDP—but in the four years up to and including 2022, it remained stuck at 2.9 per cent. There is a long way to go. The T.S.R. Subramanian Committee Report on Education Policy of 2016 also noted the low status of education in the bureaucracy and said, 'While no formal studies appear to be available, it can generally be postulated that the overall "quality" of education is a function of the [limited] political attention that the sector has received.'

There was a great deal of critical discussion and debate over RtE among activists outside parliament, and among bureaucrats, but not actually among elected politicians in the House. It was a judgement of the Supreme Court in 1993, depending on the argument that the right to life implies a right to a basic education, that stimulated civil society activism, crystallizing around the formation of the National Alliance for the Fundamental Right to Education (a network of a large number of civil society organizations) in 1998. Subsequently, in 2002, the 86th Amendment to the Constitution of India introduced Article 21A, which declares that '[t]he State shall provide free and compulsory education to all children of the age of six to fourteen years, in such manner as the State may, by law, determine'. This underlies the Right to Education Act which was passed as much as seven years later, the lengthy delay being partly due to contestation over the inclusion, or not, of pre-school education, and of post-elementary education—both, in the end, excluded from the Act.

Not only did the new laws promise social rights, they also embraced governance reform. They aimed to promote greater political transparency, responsiveness and accountability, by means of institutional mechanisms whereby ordinary people and their associations can demand accountability. This is the significance of the Right to Information Act in the context of the new rights framework, and there are transparency clauses in other parts of the rights legislation, encouraging the mobilization of people to hold the state to account, and to claim their rights as citizens. Section 17 of the National Rural Employment Guarantee Act, 2005, for example, states that 'The Gram Sabha shall conduct regular social audits of all the projects under the Scheme taken up [in the local area]'. By 'social audit' is meant a public process of reviewing official records and of establishing whether or not there is a correspondence between what is reported and what has actually happened. The Food Security Act, too, legislates for social audits of the functioning of ration shops. Such auditing was pioneered in Rajasthan by the MKSS, using the instrument of a *jan sunwai* (public hearing). In the course of events of this kind detailed accounts, derived from official expenditure records and other supporting documentation, are read aloud to assembled villagers. The fact that, in Rajasthan, the conduct of these events should have been vigorously resisted by local officials is a testament to how powerful a vehicle of accountability they can be. The principle of citizen participation is an extremely important one, promising the deepening of democracy well beyond the elections to public bodies that are held every few years.

That rights to work, to food, to education, and in the case of forest dwellers, to means of securing their livelihoods, have now been legislated for is a very major change. The implementation of them has, unsurprisingly, been uneven, not least between states. Their importance was demonstrated very clearly, however, during the Covid-19 pandemic, when very many people depended heavily upon employment under MGNREGS, and on food supplied through the Public Distribution System—the apparent reluctance of the government to supply sufficient funding for them notwithstanding. The rights to work and to food, however, in the way they have been implemented, essentially provide social protection, and in the words of a World Bank document, 'safety nets in India remain primarily "nets" rather than "ropes" or "ladders" which seek to provide sustained movement out of poverty'. Sustained improvement in well-being in India requires—it bears repetition—more investment and more attention to education and health. Neither has figured at all prominently on the agendas of politicians. And a striking feature of the rights activism in contemporary India is that there has been relatively little progress with regard to public provisioning of health care. As the Government of India's *Economic Survey 2015–16* conceded, Indians are very heavily reliant on private health care, and the country has done very poorly in regard to Universal Health Coverage (an index developed by the World Bank to measure progress in health sectors), in relation to comparator countries.

The 'new rights agenda' has, therefore, significant limitations, and Niraja Gopal Jayal's argument that it amounts to 'welfare disguised as rights' can certainly be justified. In its implementation it re-asserts categories of citizenship, distinguishing between those who rely on 'welfare' and those who do not. Just how citizens can go to law to secure their rights, in a legal system with a mammoth backlog of cases, is also far from clear—though the fact that there is a legal right may make for a point of leverage and an incentive for organization. The programmes that have been set up for the realization of the rights that have been legally recognized provide palliatives in the context of an economic system that has never reflected the intention of Article 39 when it says that the 'State shall direct its policy toward securing...that the operation of the economic system does not result in the concentration of wealth and means of production to the common detriment'. The programmes have had the effect, rather, of legitimizing the concentration of wealth and opportunity. This has been more than ever the case in the period of the BJP-led government headed by Narendra Modi since 2014—as I will argue in chapter five.

Despite the limited movement there has been towards the realization of positive freedoms, therefore, it would be generous to argue that the glass is as much as half full.

## Chapter V

# Liberty in the Time of Hindutva

It is deeply, tragically ironic, that the description of the way the British ruled their empire—through 'legalized lawlessness'—should apply quite well to the rule of post-Independence governments of India. What are the laws that have permitted these governments to detain people without trial for long periods, on suspicion that they are about to commit an illegal act, and even to presume them guilty until they can prove otherwise, but legal justifications for lawlessness? Governments have worked hard, over the years, to keep these laws and their actions above and beyond judicial scrutiny. As I have explained in chapter three, these aspects of the behaviour of Indian governments go right back to the beginning, with the passage of the Preventive Detention Act of 1950, legitimated by the Trojan Horse that is Article 22 of the Constitution—a 'Trojan Horse' because it has been an instrument for the exercise of the power of the state against Fundamental Rights.

In our present world, in India, as in many other countries, the real or supposed claims of 'security' are justifying all manner of anti-liberal or frankly autocratic measures that undermine basic freedoms. In the 'Mother of Democracies', for instance, the United Kingdom, the governments of Boris Johnson, and of his successors, have passed legislation that seriously restricts citizens' rights of protest and gives such powers to the police that even senior policemen have objected. In India, in the era of BJP-led governments since 2014, oriented towards the realization of the claims of Hindutva, 'legalized lawlessness' has gone further than ever. The context for this has included a continuing struggle between the executive and the judiciary. In the early period of the Modi government the tussle brought a prolonged, almost complete halt to the appointment of judges, as members of the bench in the Supreme Court stood up against pressures from the government. Thereafter, several CJIs appeared to be much more pliant, causing profound concerns about the independence of the judiciary.

**Article 21: Protection of Life and Personal Liberty**

It may seem far-fetched to compare the ways in which post-colonial governments of India have operated with those of the colonial rulers. When ordinary laws proved inadequate in quelling rebellion, colonial officials turned to declarations of martial law and states of emergency, which permitted sometimes terrible violence under the aegis of the state (such as happened in Jallianwala Bagh in April 1919, or when the city of Cork, in Ireland, was set ablaze in December 1920). The incremental legalizing and legitimating of state-directed violence when ordinary laws proved insufficient for maintaining control is what the historian of the British Empire, Caroline Elkins, has termed 'legalized lawlessness'. Can such an idea possibly be applied to post-colonial governments of India? Through its anti-terror legislation, however, the Indian state has given itself sweeping, unbridled and unregulated powers of search, seizure and arrest, allowed the incarceration of citizens for long periods without charge, denied them procedural rights like bail, and changed the rules of evidence with the presumption not of innocence, but of guilt. It has used (or rather mis-used) these powers very widely to quell criticism and dissent, and under them allowed the police to exercise violence not at all unlike that which was carried on under colonial rule. It is sadly the case that the Indian police force was modelled after the Royal Irish Constabulary, which functioned as an army of occupation rather than policing with the compliance of citizens. In India police brutality, and the regular use of torture by policemen, are well known, but carried on in the context of a culture of impunity in which officers are usually shielded from prosecution. The then Chief Justice of India, N.V. Ramana, was reported in 2021 as saying that '[c]ustodial torture and other police atrocities are problems which still prevail in our society'. 'Encounter killings'—extra-judicial killings—have become increasingly frequent, perhaps especially so in UP. In April 2023, a bench of the Supreme Court heard a plea that sought an enquiry into 183 encounters that had taken place up to that time since 2017, when Yogi Adityanath became chief minister of the state.

Police brutality has not often been as much on display, however, as in the response to protests against the proposed Citizenship (Amendment) Act (CAA), in 2019–20. In Muzaffarnagar in December 2019, for instance, protests against the CAA turned violent, perhaps because of the actions of agents provocateurs. In response, large numbers of Muslim men were rounded up by the police, placed in custody and subjected to regular beatings, in what was described by the activist and commentator Yogendra Yadav as a ruthless 'reign of terror'. On 15 December 2019, large numbers of police entered the campus of Jamia Millia Islamia, where students were protesting against the CAA, and among other actions, stormed the university library and ransacked parts of it. About 200 people were injured.

On other occasions—as when the Jawaharlal Nehru University endured an attack on 5 January 2020—violence was left to vigilante gangs while the police stood by. The use of vigilante groups in this way has become pervasive in BJP-ruled states, notably in the kind of cooperation that goes on between the police and cow protection gangs, the *gau rakshaks*, whose activities may be illegal, but who are seen as legitimate, as guardians of Hinduism. But there is abundant evidence, too, that during the riots that took place in North East Delhi in February 2020, some of the police actively participated in violence against Muslims. More recently, the National Human Rights Commission registered as many as 147 deaths in police custody, 1,882 deaths in judicial custody and 119 alleged extra-judicial killings in the first nine months of 2022. Sadly, legalized lawlessness does not seem at all inappropriate as a description of the action of post-colonial governments, and more than ever, of the actions of the BJP governments that have been in office since 2014.

### *The Unlawful Activities (Prevention) Act*

I referred in chapter three to Granville Austin's fear that the authority that the Constitution gave to the Government of India in regard to preventive detention was a danger to liberty, and outlined the subsequent history of the legislation that has followed from it. India's anti-terror legislation is now grounded in the Unlawful Activities (Prevention) Act (UAPA) that was first passed in 1967, as a measure against secessionism, but most recently amended, in great haste, in 2019, so as to have vested unfettered power in the central government to label anyone a 'terrorist'. It has been described as 'an all-encompassing law that gives overarching powers to the police/agencies with no protection or safeguards for the people. At a fundamental level, arguably, the UAPA violates Articles 14, 19, 20(3), 21 and 22 of the Constitution of India, besides violating Articles 10, 11 and 12 of the Universal Declaration of Human Rights Act, 1948, Article 6 of the European Convention on Human Rights, and Article 14 of the International Covenant on Civil and Political Rights. It also violates Sections 24–26 of the Indian Evidence Act'.

UAPA incorporates significant provisions from earlier legislation intended to counter terrorism. It takes over some of the wide powers that were legislated for under the Terrorist and Disruptive Activities (Prevention) Act (TADA) of 1985, and then, after TADA lapsed, that were substantially incorporated into the Prevention of Terrorism Act (POTA) of 2002. Both these acts were subjected to vigorous criticism and censured for being used against minority groups—in the way in which POTA, for instance, was invoked in Gujarat in 2002 against Muslims. Justice J.S. Verma, then chair of the National Human

Rights Commission, pointed out that 76,000 under-trials booked under TADA had little or nothing to do with 'crimes related to national security or terrorism'. There were, for instance, 20,000 in Gujarat alone, though the state had at that time experienced no terror crimes, and those detained included mainly people who had taken part in protests against government policies. POTA, too, was associated with rampant abuse, as when it was used against political opponents in states ruled by the BJP. The Act was repealed by the UPA government, as it had promised, but on the same day in 2004 many of the provisions of TADA and POTA were introduced as amendments to UAPA. Whereas both TADA and POTA were subject to review and were time limited, this is not the case with UAPA.

The Coordination of Democratic Rights Organizations (CDRO)—a union of 20 civil liberties and democratic rights organizations from across India, founded in 2007 'in the context of the violent state repression of people's movements'—has argued that '[t]he law cannot be separated from the manner of its use'. And it very clearly appears—from the 'manner of its use'—that the 'purpose of the UAPA is to allow the government to outlaw opponents or those who question the status quo'. It can do this in the first place because of the way in which an act of terror is defined. Under UAPA any physical act can be deemed a terrorist act if the government can satisfy the low threshold that it is '*likely* to threaten the unity, integrity, security or sovereignty of India', or '*likely* to strike terror in the people'. The reference to an act being 'likely' to cause terror or to threaten the integrity or sovereignty of India, clearly opens up wide scope for subjective judgement. And as has been pointed out, the definition could apply, for instance, to industrial action on the part of paramedical staff. By withholding their services it might be claimed that they would be causing 'terror in the people'.

Given this loose definition of what constitutes 'terrorism', the law then allows that any authorized officer can order searches without prior judicial warrant, and make arrests, if he has reason to believe, from 'personal knowledge or information given by any person', that a terrorist offence has been or is likely to be committed. Thereafter, the suspect/accused can be kept in detention before being charged for up to 180 days. By comparison, in the United Kingdom this period is limited to 28 days, which is already very much longer than in comparator countries. In the United States it is just 48 *hours*. Bail for persons accused of committing an offence under UAPA is effectively impossible. Bail may be denied if the court forms the opinion that there are 'reasonable grounds for believing that the accusation against the person is *prima facie* true' (or, in other words, the accusation is held to be true until it is proven otherwise). A ruling of the

Supreme Court on this in 2019 means, in effect, that all that is required for the denial of bail is a charge under UAPA and some material implicating the accused person. In a complete reversal of legal norms, the presumption of innocence is denied to the accused under UAPA. If there is some evidence, plausibly linked to the accused, then 'the Court shall assume, unless the contrary is shown, that the accused has committed such offence'. There is a presumption of guilt.

What it all means is that people accused under UAPA can remain in jail for a very long time. More than one hundred people arrested in December 2001, for instance, accused of having participated in a meeting of the banned Students' Islamic Movement of India (SIMI), were finally acquitted 19 years later, in March 2021. The judgement of the chief magistrate's court in Surat was that the investigating agencies had been unable to prove jihadi terrorist activity against them. No member of these agencies was called to question, however, for illegal police custody, fabricating or concealing evidence, or committing torture. Now, official data show a steady increase in the number of cases under UAPA—and also that only 25 to 30 per cent of them are charge-sheeted within the extended period of 180 days. There are, therefore, many lengthy incarcerations, though a high proportion of cases—75 per cent in the three years to 2016—end in acquittal.

The amendments to UAPA introduced in great haste by the Modi regime in 2019—the Bill was introduced on 8 July and came into effect on 14 August—have further increased the power of the executive. The government can now designate individuals as 'terrorists'—not just, as before, organizations—without giving them any effective redress. They are denied due judicial process. The amendments also give powers to the government to ban organizations even if it only 'believes' they are involved in terrorism. Again, given the lack of clear definitions, there is plenty of scope for the government to use the law against whomsoever it finds to be getting in its way. This was what happened to students of Jawaharlal Nehru University and Jamia Millia Islamia, and to members of Pinjra Tod (a Delhi-based women's movement) who were booked under UAPA for protesting against the Citizenship (Amendment) Act in 2020. It was also invoked against those who were protesting against the National Register of Citizens (NRC) in Assam; members of Fridays for Future, a non-governmental organization campaigning against the draft Environmental Impact Assessment notification; those who used a Virtual Private Network (VPN) in Kashmir; 11 of those accused in the Bhima Koregaon case (on which more below); and many people who were accused of being behind the Delhi riots of February 2020. Those accused over the Delhi riots did not, however, include BJP leaders like Kapil Mishra and

Anurag Thakur whose incitement of their followers to violence—for example, by describing protesters as traitors who deserved to be shot—is on record.

In June 2021, the Delhi High Court granted bail to three of the student activists who had organized protests against the CAA, and who had been arrested on multiple criminal charges, including committing terrorist acts under UAPA. The Court held:

> We are constrained to say...that in its anxiety to suppress dissent and in the morbid fear that matters may get out of hand, the state has blurred the line between the constitutionally guaranteed 'right to protest' and 'terrorist activity'. If such blurring gains traction, democracy would be in peril.

The government appealed against this ruling in the Supreme Court, which ordered that the judgement of the High Court should not be cited as a precedent—in line with the tendency for a more conservative and restricted reading of freedom of assembly.

In March 2023, the Supreme Court made it easier for the government to jail people under UAPA, when it overturned three judgements from 2011 in which it had been said that the prosecution had to show *active* membership of an 'unlawful association'—that is, that an accused person had engaged in overt acts promoting the cause of the association. Now the court ruled that simple membership of a banned organization is an offence under UAPA—though what defines 'membership' is vague. Possessing publications perhaps? Having attended a meeting? The court's ruling opens up further possibilities for a government to constrain dissenters and critics.

### *The Elgar Parishad Case*

The most notorious instance of the use of the UAPA by the Modi government to silence dissent is the case of the 16 activists, lawyers and scholars, who have been arrested—the first five of them on 6 June 2018, four in August 2018, and others in 2020—initially for their supposed responsibility for violence that took place in the village of Bhima Koregaon on 1 January 2018, but then on charges of being members of the banned Communist Party of India (Maoist) and of having plotted to overthrow the government and to assassinate the Prime Minister. They are described as 'urban Naxals' (to distinguish them from the Maoists active in rural India).

Bhima Koregaon, about 30 kilometres away from Pune, is the site of the memorial of an historic victory in 1818 of a British regiment with 500 Mahar (Dalit) soldiers over a much larger force of the Peshwa kingdom. Since the visit there of Dr Ambedkar in 1927 it has been a site of their self-assertion for Dalits. On the eve of the 200th anniversary of the battle, on 31 December 2017, members of more than 200 Dalit and other organizations came together in an event, organized by two senior lawyers, known as the Elgar Parishad (meaning 'congress for speaking aloud') that was addressed by several Dalit leaders, who were critical of the Modi regime. Then, on the following day, as large numbers of Dalits converged on Bhima Koregaon, violence broke out, one man was killed and others were injured. Subsequently there were protests all over Maharashtra, and more than 300 young Dalits were arrested. On 2 January, a first information report (FIR) was filed against two leaders of Hindutva organizations, accusing them of having instigated the violence—a case that has never been properly investigated. An FIR filed six days later, however, accusing the Elgar Parishad activists of being responsible, was taken up very actively by the Pune police, leading to a series of police raids and the seizure of electronic devices from the homes of a number of activists, including Rona Wilson and human rights lawyer Surendra Gadling, neither of whom was named in the FIR nor present at the Elgar Parishad or Bhima Koregaon events. They and three others were arrested on 6 June 2018.

The police claim that the five of them and the others accused in the Bhima Koregaon case conspired against the state relies largely on documents seized mainly from their computers. In December 2021, a digital forensic company based in the US, Arsenal Consultancy, reported that evidence collected by the National Investigation Agency was planted in attacks on the computers of Wilson, Gadling, and of the Jesuit priest and long-time tribal rights activist, Stan Swamy. Arsenal found that Wilson's computer had been hacked into for 22 months, and that Father Stan Swamy's had been compromised from October 2014 till it was seized by the Pune police in 2019. A report from December 2022, five years on from the Elgar Parishad and Bhima Koregaon events, and seven months since a special court had directed that all the evidence be copied to the accused, revealed that still 60 per cent of 'clone copies' of the evidence against the accused had not been shared with them. By that time Fr Stan Swamy was dead. Arrested in October 2020 at the age of 83, he was the oldest person to have been arrested under UAPA, and suffering from Parkinson's disease. His health deteriorated rapidly, and it appeared that he was treated with unnecessary harshness while in prison.

The Supreme Court had held a month-long hearing in September 2018 about pleas for a special investigation of the events at Bhima Koregaon and against the arrests of the rights activists. Though arguing that '[d]issent is the safety valve of democracy', the majority judgement dismissed the pleas. In a dissenting judgement, Justice D.Y. Chandrachud—who later, in November 2022, followed his father as Chief Justice of India—argued:

> Our recent decisions reiterate the value of individual dignity as essential to a democratic way of life. But lofty edicts in judicial pronouncements can have no meaning to a citizen unless the constitutional quest for human liberty translates into securing justice for individuals whose freedom is under threat in specific cases.

The death of Father Stan Swamy is a particular marker of India's descent towards 'the abyss of unrestrained power' that CJI Chandrachud's father feared.

### Article 19: Freedoms Threatened

The uses of UAPA have effectively removed one side—Article 21—of the 'golden triangle' to which the older CJI Chandrachud referred. What of the second side, Article 19? And what of that other freedom among the four distinguished by President Roosevelt, freedom of worship?

#### *Freedom of Speech and Expression*

Sadly, the concerns that were expressed by members of the Constituent Assembly about the way in which the freedoms specified in Article 19 were made subject to various conditions have been proven all too justified. Think of the remarks of Somnath Lahiri, the communist member, in the debate on the Interim Report on Fundamental Rights, quoted in chapter three. He expressed the fear that he might find himself in jail for having made a critical remark about the government. He worried that repressive colonial laws, including the law regarding sedition—referring to words, signs or images that are intended to excite 'disaffection' toward the government—remained in place. He worried, too, about whether the freedom of the press was sufficiently protected. On all counts, the situation has become worse than Lahiri might have imagined—even though the law against sedition has been suspended since May 2022.

It is now quite commonplace for those who have been critical in some way, especially of political leaders, to be arrested, often drawing on very dubious interpretations of the law. There are many examples. Two of them concern arrests made in UP in 2022. Five men were arrested, for instance, for having put up a hoarding showing Narendra Modi offering a cooking gas cylinder for Rs 1,105—then the highest ever price—with other critical text, under the hashtag #ByeByeModi. Local BJP leaders registered a case with the police, on the claim that the action was prejudicial to national integration and 'promoted enmity, hatred or ill-will between classes'. The relevance of these accusations to the action is very doubtful. Then, a schoolboy was arrested for having posted an 'offensive' image of Chief Minister Adityanath, though it might have been better described merely as 'silly'. It was argued by Siddharth Varadarajan in an article—entitled 'Freedom of Expression is Dead in

India'—to have been quite harmless by comparison with a Shankar cartoon from 1953 showing a naked Nehru unsuccessfully imploring the United Nations, for which the cartoonist won a complimentary word from the prime minister. Perhaps the most egregious case of all, however, is that of Rahul Gandhi, who was convicted by a court in Surat in March 2023 for defamation, and sentenced to two years' imprisonment, for a remark made at an election rally in 2019 in which he spoke of several individuals named Modi, including the prime minister, as well as two notable men with serious criminal charges hanging over them, as 'thieves'. An FIR was filed by a BJP MLA in Gujarat claiming that the 'Modi community' had been defamed. That Gandhi should have been convicted was found more than surprising by lawyers, since those bearing the name 'Modi' are not a 'collection of persons' as understood in law. But Gandhi was immediately disqualified from Parliament. This came very shortly after he had spoken at Cambridge University about democracy being under attack in India. The defamation law is a threat to the freedom of speech and expression and has long been used against the press in India.

Criticism of the government is now routinely described as 'anti-national', and—until its suspension in May 2022—opened up the possibility of a charge under the law against sedition, a colonial legacy dating back more than 150 years. It was described by a former CJI in February 2023 as 'a thorn in the flesh for journalistic ventures'. But in recent years it has not only been journalists who have been accused under this law. A sedition case was filed, for instance, against a school for having staged a play that was anti-CAA. Another case that became internationally well known was that of a young environmental activist, Disha Ravi, who was arrested in February 2021 for her alleged involvement with an online toolkit put out by Greta Thunberg and having to do with the ongoing farmer protests. This was said to be a form of sedition.

In the Constituent Assembly it wasn't only Somnath Lahiri who was anxious that reference to 'sedition' should not be included among the provisos attaching to the freedom of speech and expression. The conservative K.M. Munshi spoke against it in the debate on the Draft Constitution (on 1 December 1948), and in the end the word did not appear in the Constitution. But the law against sedition has continued in use. Under the UPA governments headed by Manmohan Singh there were on average 62 cases each year; the Modi government saw an average of just under 80 cases a year between 2014 and February 2021. In an affidavit submitted to the Supreme Court by the government, Prime Minister Modi was quoted as saying of the law that it is 'colonial baggage that has passed its utility'. The court suspended the law, but subsequently a report of the Law Commission of India argued that the law was 'imperative' for safeguarding 'the unity and integrity of the nation'—which it held to be inadequately protected by the UAPA. The Commission recommended that the relevant section of the Indian Penal Code should remain 'draconian', penalizing 'disaffection' with government, and 'disloyalty'.

There were other members of the Constituent Assembly who agreed with Lahiri's view that the freedom of the press 'has been crushed completely...[and]...in a free India in order that people may feel freedom and act up to it, there should not be such drastic curtailment of liberties of the press'. But then he worried that there was 'not even a mention of the liberty of the press in this whole list of fundamental rights submitted by the Committee...' In response, it was pointed out that curtailment of the freedom of the press could not be consistent with what the Constitution had to say about the freedom of speech and of expression, so that there was no need for a distinct article. Technically correct, no doubt, but still, the so-called 'fourth estate' has always had a struggle in independent India. Speaking truth to power is always a precarious business. In 2023, in the index of press freedom, prepared by the respected international organization, Reporters Without Borders, India ranked 161 out of 180 countries. It was noted that 'all the mainstream media are now owned by wealthy businessmen close to Narendra Modi'—this following the effective takeover of the once fiercely independent NDTV by Gautam Adani in 2022, while India's other outstanding multi-billionaire business owner, Mukesh Ambani, was said to own 70 media outlets catering to 800 million Indians. Reporters Without Borders also said, 'Modi has an army of supporters who track down all online reporting regarded as critical of the government and wage horrific harassment campaigns against the sources...many journalists are, in practice, forced to censor themselves.'

The RSS and the BJP recognized the significance and the potential of digital media at a very early stage. An 'IT shakha' was established in Bangalore as early as 2001, and an army of social media correspondents was set up to engage in a form of moral policing. Online trolls exalt Prime Minister Modi, while purveying Islamophobia and attacking so-called 'sickularists'. Many often target journalists, posting fake messages and going after women journalists—such as Barkha Dutt, for 21 years with NDTV, and a very well-known media figure—with threats of gang rape. Trolls welcomed the murder in 2017 of the Karnataka journalist Gauri Lankesh, who was staunchly secular and a well-known critic of Hindu nationalist politics. Though the case remains unproven, there is evidence that the Sanatan Sanstha, a fringe organization supportive of Hindutva—though not formally affiliated with the Sangh

Parivar—was responsible for this murder and that of four other noted 'liberals'. The Anti-Terrorism Squad of Maharashtra had sought to have the organization banned, but it was declared not to be a terrorist organization by the Bombay High Court in March 2023. It is, said the court, a charitable trust aiming to impart spiritual knowledge—exactly as it claims on its website.

There are more instances of the harassment of journalists than can possibly be summarized. As the well-known historian and commentator Ramachandra Guha has said on several occasions, he himself, and others like him, such as the writer Arundhati Roy, who work in English and who have international reputations, may be left free to criticize the government. This is far from the case, however, for less well-known, local journalists, writing in Hindi and regional languages. There are a good many cases of the use of UAPA against journalists, as in that of Siddique Kappan, who was finally released in 2023 after having been jailed for more than two years. He had been arrested while travelling to Hathras in UP, to cover the infamous gang rape and murder of a young Dalit woman, and he was accused of seeking to incite caste violence. Another notable case is that of Irfan Mehraj, a Kashmiri journalist associated with the human rights activist Khurram Parvaz, himself arrested in 2021 under anti-terrorism laws. It was reported that at least 55 journalists faced arrest or other threats for their critical reporting during the Covid-19 pandemic, one of them, in UP, for 'maligning the image of the Chief Minister'. Media organizations such as *The Wire*, and individuals like Prannoy Roy, the co-founder of NDTV, even though they work in English, have been subjected to intimidating raids by government agencies under one pretext or another. Three major newspaper groups have faced declining advertising revenues because of government cutting advertisements through them.

There is, in short, abundant evidence that the freedom of speech and expression, the first of the freedoms specified in Article 19, and for long subject to constraint—beginning with the 1st Amendment—has become ever more threatened in the period of the ascendancy of the BJP under the leadership of Narendra Modi. Latterly the government has taken steps to ensure its capacity to censor the internet as well, and since 2016 India has accounted for 58 per cent of all internet shutdowns across the world. Over 55,000 websites have been blocked since January 2015, most of them 'to protect the Indian state'. Again, there is evidence of the selective use of the powers of censorship, as when members of the ruling party have been allowed to remain on social media platforms despite violating hate speech rules.

***Freedom of Assembly; Freedom of Association***

A recent independent report on the right to peaceful assembly in India reaches the unhappy conclusion that 'there is a disturbing trend of growing intolerance toward democratic processes and social movements in India, where inconvenience to everyday life caused by peaceful public protests receives greater attention than the protection and promotion of rights'. It is no compensation to know that exactly the same can be said of the United Kingdom.

The freedom of assembly is of fundamental importance for a democracy, and the ideals of the Constitution expressed in the Preamble, those of Liberty, Equality, Fraternity and the pursuit of Justice, cannot possibly be realized if people are unable to assemble—to meet—in order to discuss and debate, and to advocate and to try to influence matters that affect their lives. India, of course, has a rich history of public protest, most recently displayed in the resistance of farmers to policies that the government sought to impose by fiat. There is a great history, too, of contestation of ideas—as was so clearly shown in the Constituent Assembly debates. But the space for dissent and for diversity of views in the country has decidedly shrunk, as this chapter has shown. The freedom of assembly is a fundamental human right under the Universal Declaration of Human Rights, but it has come increasingly under threat in India, as the discussion of the way the UAPA is being used clearly shows. The words of the Delhi High Court, quoted earlier, sum it up very well: 'the state has blurred the line between the constitutionally guaranteed "right to protest" and "terrorist activity"'. An increasingly pliant judiciary has been inclined to support the government. A ruling, for example, of the Supreme Court of February 2021 was:

> The right to protest cannot be any time and everywhere. There may be some spontaneous protests, but in case of prolonged dissent or protest [exactly as happened in Shaheen Bagh, in Delhi, in the opposition to the CAA], there cannot be continued occupation of public place...

Article 19 states that the right to peaceable assembly is subject to any law that imposes 'reasonable restrictions' on it, 'in the interests of the sovereignty and integrity of India, or public order'. The last, 'public order', has increasingly been taken to mean that the public must not be inconvenienced, and successive governments have, often, abridged the right of assembly. Each state has its own laws about policing and public order. All accord power overwhelmingly to the executive and to the police. The discussion earlier in this chapter shows how this power is used, in effect to deny the right to assembly and to crush protest.

The French writer Alexis de Tocqueville, who studied

democracy in America in the 1830s, was perhaps the first to show the importance of a vigorous civil society for democracy, and it is an argument that has been effectively proven across the world. Voluntary associations in civil society, and non-governmental organizations, play positive roles both as monitors and critics of how governments operate, while in some circumstances they may be able to provide services to citizens more effectively than governments can. India, particularly since Mrs Gandhi's Emergency, has had a very active civil society, founded on the right to freedom of association—a right which, according to the Constitution, may be limited by 'reasonable restrictions' having to do with the 'sovereignty and integrity of India, or public order, or morality'. Ostensible concerns about sovereignty and the integrity of India have driven the erosion of the freedom of association through law that targets foreign-funded NGOs on the ground that they are instruments for foreign influence on domestic affairs and public opinion. A favourite justification for action against critical voices within civil society on the part of right-wing nationalist regimes across the world is that they are 'foreign agents'.

The space for civil society has been progressively squeezed by successive governments, and more by the Modi governments than by those of the UPA. The UPA took a strategic position in regard to civil society, being supportive and attentive in some connections, and hostile in some others. Governments headed by Manmohan Singh had an adversarial relationship with some NGOs—human rights and environmental organizations in the main—but positive relationships with others. The governments headed by Narendra Modi, on the other hand, have generally sought to close the civil society space, except where it is occupied by organizations that have some affiliation with the Sangh Parivar. Research has shown that the BJP has won electoral support among tribal people, for example, in some parts of the country, at least in part because of the activities of voluntary service organizations affiliated with the RSS.

The instrument for the pushback against civil society has been the 'weaponizing' of tax regulations and the Foreign Contributions (Regulation) Act (FCRA). According to a statement in the Lok Sabha by a minister in December 2022, the FCRA licences of 6,677 organizations were cancelled between 2017 and 2021. Three months later the same minister reported that 1,827 licences had been cancelled in 'the last five years'. He also informed parliament that there were 16,383 FCRA-registered organizations as of 10 March 2023. The difference between the figures that were given is puzzling, but it is clear that the numbers of cancelled licences are substantial and represent a significant proportion of registered organizations. They include a number of high-profile cases, including those of Amnesty India, which halted its operations altogether in 2020, Greenpeace India, which had its accounts frozen in 2015, the Rajiv Gandhi Foundation, Oxfam India and the Centre for Policy Research. But there are very many other, less well-known organizations, including a good many environmental organizations, whose activities have been reduced or stopped altogether because of the withdrawal of their FCRA certification.

The erosion of the freedoms of speech and expression, of assembly and of association, show that the second side of the 'golden triangle', Article 19, has also been effectively taken away. But other freedoms, too, are threatened.

### Article 25: Freedom of Religion

As I started writing this part of the chapter I came across the following news item:

> A Muslim labourer was assaulted and forced to chant 'Jai Shri Ram' by three men in UP's Bulandshahr last week. Sahil was accused of theft, tied to a tree and beaten up. The assailants also shaved his head partially, and made a video of the assault. The incident came to light after the video was shared widely on social media...

It is a sad reflection of these times that one reaction is to think that Sahil was at least fortunate that he was not lynched. There have been so many cases of lynching, most commonly of Muslims, and over accusations of killing cows or transporting them for slaughter. In a particularly notorious incident, in September 2015, Mohammed Akhlaq was lynched in a village in western UP, following the broadcasting of messages by a local temple that he and his family had slaughtered cattle and were storing beef. Meat was found in Akhlaq's refrigerator, which later tests showed, however, to be mutton.

News items like the one I have quoted appear almost every day. A few days before the story of Sahil came the first reports that Muslims in the town of Purola in Uttarakhand were being subjected to a concerted campaign by Hindutva groups to force them to leave. There have been many cases, too, of bulldozers being used to demolish homes and property of citizens, mostly Muslim, accused of rioting or of participation in protests, even before a court has convicted them, in UP, MP, Gujarat and Delhi. The official explanation is that they are encroachments or 'illegal constructions'—charges which are extremely difficult to prove or disprove. Twelve eminent lawyers wrote to the then CJI N.V. Ramana, calling demolitions in UP a form of 'collective extra-judicial punishment', and violation of international law. But in UP the bulldozer has become a cultural icon. The chief minister has been referred to as 'Bulldozer Baba'.

There is overwhelming evidence that such violent

discrimination against Muslims is widespread and of frequent occurrence. It is encouraged by such arguments as this one, in the annual report of the RSS, released at its conclave in Ahmedabad in March 2022:

> There appear to be elaborate plans by a particular community to enter the government machinery. Behind all this, it seems that a long-term goal is working... All-out efforts, with organized strength, awakening and activeness to defeat this menace...is the need of the hour.

The 'particular community' doesn't need to be named. The claim that is made about it seems flatly to fly in the face of facts: that there is no Muslim member in the ruling party in the Lok Sabha, and that there is clear evidence that Muslims are under-represented in government services. The RSS is much more circumspect in its statements, however, than some Hindu religious leaders, like Yati Narsinghanand Saraswati, who describes Muslims as 'demons', and calls for an India 'free of Islam'. This was the context for the argument of a group of 108 former senior officials who wrote a letter to the prime minister just a month after the RSS conclave, in which they spoke of the 'escalation of hate violence against minority communities, particularly Muslims, in the last few years and across several states... [having] acquired a frightening new dimension'.

Christians, too, are subject to attack and discrimination.

The government told the Supreme Court that allegations in a petition calling for a probe into attacks on Christians, were based on 'falsehoods'. Yet, as many as 302 attacks against Christians took place in the first seven months of 2022, according to the United Christian Forum—the figure being based on the number of distress calls received by the organization's helplines. Christians may be especially targeted in the ten states that have passed anti-conversion laws. These generally ban 'forceful' or 'fraudulent' conversion, and Uttarakhand, Himachal Pradesh and UP impose a ban as well specifically on conversion through marriage. These laws are often the basis for false accusations, harassment and violence that occur with impunity. Propagation of one's religion is a fundamental right under Article 25 of the Constitution, together with freedom of conscience and free profession and practice of religion. Propagation may, of course, lead to others wishing to convert to the faith in question, but then accusations of the use of force or incentives can easily be made. Courts will not always find as did the Bombay High Court in May 2023 that a Christian couple, accused of religious conversion, had exercised their right to propagate their faith, but without there being evidence of forcible conversion. The freedom to practise one's faith, too, is questioned, as in the case of the college girls in Karnataka who were stopped from attending classes because of wearing the hijab. When six of them challenged, through the courts, a government order banning the hijab, they were described as 'terrorists' by a BJP leader. The ban was upheld by the Karnataka High Court which held that wearing hijab is not essential to Islam. The girls' fundamental right to practise their religion was surely brought into question by the ruling.

There is, therefore, abundant evidence that Article 25 of the Constitution is being eroded all the time, as the members of religious minorities are subjected to violent discrimination, and are not protected as they should be, by the state. Article 15, on 'Prohibition of discrimination', is clearly threatened. Freedom of conscience and free profession and practice of religion means that people should be free to make choices about their faith, but this fundamental freedom is threatened by anti-conversion laws. Another, related, fundamental personal freedom is the right to choose one's marriage partner, and this too is threatened. There are many cases of couples being subjected to attack in cross-caste and cross-faith marriages, encouraged in the case of marriages between Muslim men and Hindu women by the campaign against the so-called 'love-jihad', set up by the chief minister of UP, Yogi Adityanath, among others. This rests on the baseless claim that Muslim men are luring Hindu women into marriage and forcing them to convert. It is understandable, then, that the decision of the Government of Maharashtra, in December 2022, to set up an 'Inter-caste/Interfaith Marriage Family Coordination Committee' was widely perceived as threatening. It was said to have been set up to gather information, but also to provide 'a platform for women who have been estranged from their families'. It was not encouraging that the committee was to be headed by a BJP minister who had earlier called for 'capital punishment for killers of cows'.

**Positive Freedoms**

The conclusion of chapter four, on positive freedoms, is that there was some movement toward their realization in the 'new rights agenda' that was advanced in the time of the UPA government after 2004—though sometimes in the face of opposition from powerful voices within the government. But I also noted that the implementation of the rights to work and (so far as it had gone) to food, and to other social security measures, provided for palliatives in the context of an economic system that had brought greater concentrations of wealth and opportunity—in direct contravention of Article 39 and the spirit of the Directive Principles in general. The pursuit of economic growth, as the priority above all, has rarely been questioned. What has happened subsequently, in the time of the dominance of Hindu nationalist politics?

This is not the place for a thorough-going analysis of the trends in India's economic development, a task which has been made more difficult by the government's interventions in the collection, analysis and publication of critically important data. These have made tracing the trends both in economic growth and in poverty and well-being problematic. It must suffice to say that there is little room for doubt that in the aftermath of the Covid-19 pandemic India is more unequal than ever, with the livelihoods of a large swathe of those who are thought of as being 'middle class', as well of working classes, being ever more precarious. It has become increasingly obvious that worthwhile jobs are not being created at anything like the rate that is necessary, even while there are shortages in the numbers of adequately educated and trained people in some activities. There are no signs at all of any attempt having been made to realize the principles set out in Part IV of the Constitution.

When Narendra Modi, at the head of the BJP, came to power in 2014 it was thought possible that the rights agenda would be undone. Modi had, after all, mocked the employment guarantee as a 'living monument' to many years of Congress failure. But as it turned out the years of the first Modi government, to 2019, saw the gradual undermining of social rights rather than a direct attack upon them. A letter from 250 parliamentarians and other prominent public figures to the prime minister in January 2019 spoke of the employment guarantee scheme having been starved of funds. At the same time it was said that the Food Security Act was being killed by neglect. Promised maternity benefits had been whittled down. The argument of the government was that 'entitlement' was being shifted to 'empowerment', with the intention of replacing the range of welfare programmes by direct cash transfers, made into accounts newly opened for people under a scheme associated with the prime minister—the Pradhan Mantri Jan Dhan Yojana (the 'Prime Minister's People Money Scheme')—with access to their money made possible by using their mobile phones and their biometric identities (Aadhaar). It was what was called, with much fanfare, the 'JAM Scheme' (for its key components, Jan Dhan-Aadhaar-Mobile). It was argued that this would empower people, by giving them choice, while being much more efficient through reducing possibilities for corruption, leakage and waste. The transfers would be much better targeted (though on what basis was never made clear). The arguments in favour of direct cash transfers were found persuasive by many, though as the commentator Pratap Bhanu Mehta wrote, there is a danger that cash transfer becomes seen 'as a substitute for governance rather than an instrument of governance. It gives up on the state'.

Mehta was perhaps proven right by the trends in

government policy, at least in so far as it has actually given priority to the efficient delivery of material goods for people—which has proven electorally very effective—rather than taking up the very much more administratively challenging task of improving the delivery of public services in education and health care, and food security. There has been a focus on the construction of toilets, under the Swachh Bharat Abhiyan, the provision of housing, under the Pradhan Mantri Gramin Awas Yojana, and on the supply of cooking gas cylinders, under the Pradhan Mantri Ujjwala Yojana, together with the supply of electricity, drinking water and rural roads. It is noticeable that the schemes are associated with the prime minister; his picture very frequently appears in connection with them. They have, no doubt, contributed to building and maintaining his popularity, as shown by polling data. To say that these schemes have served to legitimate the regime is not to deny that they have delivered real benefits to large numbers of people—even if there are many toilets that have not been properly constructed or are not properly used; houses, similarly, that haven't been properly constructed; and cooking gas cylinders that are no longer being filled because the gas is so expensive. But do they empower people and increase opportunity for them in the way that good quality public education and accessible public health care would? These remain lacking, and so long as they are lacking, the aim that Nehru set out all those years ago, when he spoke of 'real freedom', cannot be realized.

The unhappy conclusion of this chapter, and of this book, is that the realization of liberty in the fuller sense that was envisaged by the Founders, and set out in the programme of social transformation of Parts III and IV of the Constitution, has been set back in the early years of the 21st century. The seamless web of the Constitution of which Granville Austin wrote has been badly torn.

# Afterword

As I sat down to write this Afterword news came through that a bench of the Supreme Court had ordered the release on bail of the rights activists Vernon Gonsalves and Arun Ferreira who had been arrested more than five years before, for their alleged role in the Elgar Parishad case. The justices on the bench observed that the material evidence available 'does not justify their continuous detention' (*The Wire*, 28 July 2023). The judiciary continues to exercise some restraint, therefore, on the exercise of arbitrary power by the executive. But while the fact that Indian society has not quite slipped into the 'abyss' that CJI Chandrachud feared is a matter of relief, it does not make up for the fact that these two men, in common with so many others, should have lost their liberty for so long. That the state can jail people for long periods on the basis only of 'suspicion', and on the presumption of guilt, is a marker of how far the Indian state has fallen away from the ideal of liberty promised in the Constitution. As I have argued in this book, this has come about in significant part because of the latitude that has been allowed the government in the exercise of powers of preventive detention, thanks in large measure to Article 22. A first step that needs to be taken in order to reverse this is the notification, after more than forty years, of section 3 of the 44th Amendment of 1978, exactly as the group of former senior civil servants argued in their open letter to the law minister in October 2021. This would amend Article 22(4) and require independent judicial review of preventive detention orders, deleting the provision authorizing preventive detention without obtaining the approval of an Advisory Board. But this would just be a start. An essential further step—though one that will, no doubt, be extremely difficult to bring about—is to implement reform of policing so as to check the kind of more or less 'legalized lawlessness' of the police that has become more and more evident.

If India has slipped some way from the negative freedom that obtains when citizens are free from despotic or autocratic control, the country has also not yet advanced very far towards positive freedom, or, in other words, the 'real freedom' advocated at the very beginning of the deliberations of the Constituent Assembly. For every Indian to have the 'opportunity to develop himself according to his capacity', as Nehru had hoped for, requires, for sure, what Roosevelt referred to as freedom from want. Here India has, no doubt, made considerable progress. Yet it is still the case, according to careful research studies such as those of Anirudh Krishna, that very many Indians still move in and out of poverty, in part because they lack productive employment. But it is also the case, as Krishna expresses it in the title of his 2017 book, that the 'ladder' of economic and social mobility is broken—because of the failures of successive governments in regard to quality education and decent health care. Without massive improvements in employment, education and health, the successful economic growth that is forecast for India over the years to the one hundredth anniversary of the coming into force of the Constitution will be meaningless for very many Indians.

# Notes on Sources

## *Preface*

The classic study of the writing of the Constitution to which I refer is that of Granville Austin, *The Indian Constitution: Cornerstone of a Nation* (Oxford University Press, 1966).

## Chapter One

Quentin Skinner, 'Classical Liberty and the Coming of the English Civil War', in Martin van Gelderen and Quentin Skinner (eds), *Republicanism*, Vol. 2: *The Values of Republicanism in Early Modern Europe: A Shared European Heritage* (Cambridge University Press, 2002); Eric Hobsbawm, *The Age of Revolution 1789-1848* (first published in 1962); Christopher J. Bayly, *Recovering Liberties: Indian Thought in the Age of Liberalism and Empire* (Cambridge University Press, 2012); 'The Economist at 175: Reinventing Liberalism for the 21st Century', *The Economist*, 13 September 2018; G.B. Shaw on 'Socialism and Liberty', in *The Intelligent Woman's Guide to Socialism, Capitalism, Sovietism and Fascism* (1928); Granville Austin, *Working a Democratic Constitution: A History of the Indian Experience* (Oxford University Press, 1999).

I have taken the reference to 'fancy, modern notions' from Simon Schama's book on the French revolution, *Citizens*; the felicitous phrase 'hardly arrived in the mail, from overseas' is Ananya Vajpeyi's, in an essay for *Seminar* in 2010. I quote from Karl Polanyi, *The Great Transformation: the Political and Economic Origins of Our Time* Beacon Press (1944).

**Chapter Two**

All the documents referred to in this chapter are easily accessed at https://www.constitutionofindia.net/. The quote on the 'ironic location' of Article 22 among the fundamental rights comes from the article 'Improving Preventive Detention Laws' by John Sebastian and Faiza Rahman, published by *The India Forum* in June 2023. Harsh Mander's discussion of fraternity is in his article 'Fraternity: the Missing Link of India's Democracy', *The India Forum*, 13 February 2019. The books referred to are: Pranab Bardhan, *A World of Insecurity: Democratic Disenchantment in Rich and Poor Countries* (Harvard University Press, 2022); and Martin Wolf, *The Crisis of Democratic Capitalism* (Allen Lane, 2023).

**Chapter Three**

I have referred extensively to the two books of Granville Austin, *The Indian Constitution: Cornerstone of a Nation*, as in the Preface; and, as in chapter one, *Working a Democratic Constitution*. Also to Madhav Khosla, *India's Founding Moment: The Constitution of a Most Surprising Democracy* (Harvard University Press, 2020); to the article on 'Improving Preventive Detention Laws' by Sebastian and Rahman (as in chapter two);

and to Ujjwal Kumar Singh, 'Federalism, democracy and the national security state in India', *Territory, Politics, Governance*, vol. 10 no. 1 (2022), pp. 51-66.

The Open Letter concerning the notification of the 44th Amendment, section 3 is available at: https://constitutionalconduct.com/2021/10/16/open-letter-to-the-minister-of-law-and-justice-government-of-india-notification-of-s-3-of-the-constitution-forty-fourth-amendment-act-1978-to-provide-for-impartial-and-independ/, last accessed 31 January 2024.

***Intermezzo***

I have quoted from a classic article by M.N. Srinivas, 'The Social System of a Mysore Village', in M. Marriott (ed.), *Village India: Studies in the Little Community* (University of Chicago Press, 1955); and from M.E. Opler and R.D. Singh, 'Economic, Social and Political Change in a Village of North Central India', *Human Organization*, Summer 1952, pp. 5-12. I have drawn on O. Mendelsohn, 'The transformation of authority in rural India', *Modern Asian Studies*, vol. 27, no. 4 (1993), pp. 805–42. Anirudh Krishna's book, *The Broken Ladder: The Paradox and the Potential of India's One Billion* (Penguin Random House India, 2017), is an excellent, readable, source on the lack of opportunity for most Indians, especially those living in rural India. On 'footloose labour' and the conditions of neo-bondage that many face, the work of Jan Breman is indispensable. On 'incivility' and the findings of recent village research see Edward Simpson et al., 'A Brief History of Incivility in Rural Postcolonial India: Caste, Religion, and Anthropology', *Comparative Studies in Society and History*, vol. 60, no. 1 (2018), pp. 58-89. F.G. Bailey's work on village politics in the early years of independent India is foundational; see his *Politics and Social Change: Orissa in 1959* (University of California Press, 1963). *Mafia Raj: The Rule of Bosses in South Asia*, is the title of their book by Lucia Michelutti and her co-authors (Stanford University Press, 2019; Speaking Tiger, 2023).

**Chapter Four**

The books by Granville Austin, and by Madhav Khosla, referred in chapter three, have been of value in this chapter as well. The main sources, however, are Niraja Gopal Jayal, *Citizenship and its Discontents: An Indian History* (Permanent Black, 2013); and John Harriss, Craig Jeffrey and Trent Brown, *India: Continuity and Change in the Twenty First Century* (Polity Press, 2020), chapter 8. I have referred as well to Neera Chandhoke's article, 'The antecedents of social rights in India', in Udit Mehta (ed.), *The Indian Constituent Assembly* (Routledge, 2018).

**Chapter Five**

The idea of 'legalized lawlessness' comes from Caroline Elkins, *Legacy of Violence: A History of the British Empire* (Alfred A. Knopf, 2022). Useful sources are: Ravi Nair, 'The Unlawful Activities (Prevention) Act 2008: Repeating Past Mistakes', *Economic and Political Weekly*, 24 January 2009; and V. Suresh (of the People's Union for Civil Liberties), 'UAPA: Law as Instrumentality of State Tyranny and Violence', in the PUCL publication, *Sudha Bharadwaj Speaks*, January 2021.

The lengthy quote concerning UAPA is taken from Teesta Setalvad, 'UAPA: Terror and the Law', *Frontline*, 11 July 2021; other material taken from Venkitesh Ramakrishnan and Divya Trivedi, 'Retreat of Democracy: The terror of laws', *Frontline*, 21 March 2021. CJI Ramana's statement was reported in *The Guardian*, 10 August 2021. The 'reign of terror' in Muzaffarnagar was reported by Hannah Ellis-Petersen, *The Guardian*, 13 January 2020. See also Umang Poddar and Zafar Aafaq, 'Guilt by Association', *Scroll.in*, 7 April 2023. On Bhima Koregaon, the PUCL; and Sonam Saigal, in *The Hindu*, 30 December 2022. Siddharth Varadarajan's article, 'The Evidence is in: Freedom of Expression is Dead in India', appeared in *The Wire*, 15 July 2022. On the Law Commission Report, see K. Raj, 'Sedition Law Report: A regressive step by Law Commission', *Frontline*, 8 June 2023. Material on the media, and on the murder of Gauri Lankesh is drawn from Christophe Jaffrelot, *Modi's India: Hindu Nationalism and the Rise of Ethnic Democracy* (Princeton University Press, 2021); and on government censorship of the internet from articles in *Frontline* and *Scroll.in*. On the right to assembly I have referred to Vrinda Grover, *Assessing India's Legal Framework on the Right to Peaceful Assembly* (International Centre for Non-Profit Law, December 2021). The Bulandshahr case was reported by *Scroll.in*, 19 June 2023; and the Purola case on 13 June 2023. On 'bulldozer raj', see Tushar Mittal, 'Theatre of Destruction', *The Caravan*, 15 May 2023. The RSS statement is cited in D.K. Jha, 'Back to Basics: Has the RSS revived Golwalkar's plan for Muslims?', *The Caravan*, 30 March 2022. The letter from 108 senior officials was reported by *The Indian Express*, 27 April

2022. On violence against Christians, see Sumedha Pal, 'Over 300 attacks on Christians', *The Wire*, 7 September 2022. On positive freedoms, I have drawn largely on parts of chapter 8 of Harriss, Jeffrey and Brown, *India: Continuity and Change*, as in chapter four.

### Afterword

Anirudh Krishna's *The Broken Ladder* is referred to in the Intermezzo.

ALSO IN THIS SERIES

# SECULARISM

## How India Reshaped the Idea

*Nalini Rajan*

Secularism emerged in 17th-century Europe as an essential element of what became the modern state. The separation of church and state that it entailed paved the way for the democratic republics we take for granted today. Tolerance, as understood in the West, was sought to be introduced as state policy by the British in India too. But our nationalist leaders understood their country better than to adopt the concept without local adjustments.

Political philosopher Nalini Rajan examines the tension between religious freedom and state intervention in India, a tension that comes with the idea of 'principled' state intervention in matters of religion, as mandated by the Constitution. Demands for reservations and separate electorates by minorities in the early twentieth century had essentially ruled out absolute state neutrality in this respect. But it is only by analysing the fascinating debates on secularism in the Constituent Assembly (1946–49) that we see how and why the specific provisions on minority rights—Articles 25 to 30—came to be adopted. These provisions implicitly envisioned a key role for the judiciary. A full section of this book is thus devoted to understanding the role that the courts have played in establishing, and just as importantly, defining Indian secularism—through such judgements as in the Shirur Mutt case of 1954, the Durgah Committee case of 1961, the Satsangi case of 1966, the Stanislaus case of 1977, the Shah Bano case of 1985, the so-called 'Hindutva' cases of 1996, the Vaishno Devi case of 1997, and the Puttaswamy case of 2017.

This exhaustive monograph should be read by all those interested in understanding how a distinctive secularism shaped modern India, and how the latter shaped our secularism.

ALSO IN THIS SERIES

# FRATERNITY

## Constitutional Norm and Human Need

*Rajmohan Gandhi*

There's no dearth of references to a sense of kinship beyond one's family or tribe in ancient Indian texts. We know from anecdotes in the *Ramayana* and *Mahabharata*, the Upanishads and epigraphic sources like Ashoka's 12th Major Rock Edict, that our ancestors were no strangers to an expansive understanding of fraternity. Therefore, although the earliest adoption of fraternity as state motto happened in 18th-century France, the West cannot claim to have taught fraternity to India. Even so, it took our freedom struggle and the writing of the Constitution for it to become an integral value governing our lives.

While the idea of fraternity was implicit in the Motilal Nehru Constitutional Draft of 1928 and the 1931 Karachi Resolution of the Indian National Congress, the National Movement's commitment to it was questioned by leaders like Dr Babasaheb Ambedkar because the Movement appeared to prioritize the anti-colonial struggle over social reform to eliminate caste inequality. Dr Ambedkar, who had suffered caste oppression, knew that there couldn't be a democratic future if caste wasn't done away with. However, his antagonism with Mahatma Gandhi, the pre-eminent leader of the National Movement, is often amplified. This monograph argues, instead, that not only did both hold each other in high regard, it was due to Ambedkar's steadfast opposition to caste that, through Gandhi, modern Indian society learnt to take its first steps towards embodying fraternity, even as it fought the Raj.

Rajmohan Gandhi, one of India's leading and most admired thinkers, moves easily from ancient India to modern Europe to an intimate portrait of the epic face-off between Gandhi and Ambedkar which led to the Poona Pact of 1932. This engaging monograph should be read by everyone invested in upholding the constitutional norm of fraternity in our increasingly divided country.